MW00677787

The Everyday Atheist

Some Other Titles From New Falcon Publications

Aleister Crowley's Illustrated Goetia
Taboo: Sex, Religion & Magick
Sex Magic, Tantra & Tarot: The Way of the Secret Lover
    By Christopher S. Hyatt, Ph.D., and Lon Milo DuQuette
Ask Baba Lon
    By Lon Milo DuQuette
Enochian World of Aleister Crowley
    By Lon Milo DuQuette and Aleister Crowley,
    Edited by David Cherubim
Cosmic Trigger 1
Cosmic Trigger 2
Cosmic Trigger 3
Coincidance
The Earth Will Shake
Email to the Universe
Nature's God
Prometheus Rising
TSOG: The Thing that Ate the Constitution
Wilhelm Reich in Hell
The Widow's Son
The Walls Came Tumbling Down
Sex, Drugs & Magick
Quantum Psychology
    By Robert Anton Wilson
Info-Psychology
The Intelligence Agents
Neuropolitique
What Does WoMan Want?
    By Timothy Leary, Ph.D.
Healing Energy, Prayer and Relaxation
The Complete Golden Dawn System of Magic
The Golden Dawn Audio CDs
What You Should Know About The Golden Dawn
The Eye in the Triangle: An Interpretation of Aleister Crowley
    By Israel Regardie
Rebellion, Revolution and Religiousness
    By Osho
The Dream Illuminati
The Illuminati of Immortality
    By Wayne Saalman
Monsters & Magical Sticks
    By Steven Heller, Ph.D. & Terry Steele
An Insider's Guide to Robert Anton Wilson
    Eric Wagner
Shaping Formless Fire
    By Stephen Mace
Aleister Crowley and the Treasure House of Images
    By J.F.C. Fuller, Aleister Crowley, David Cherubim,
    Lon Milo DuQuette and Nancy Wasserman

Please visit our website at http://www.newfalcon.com

The Everyday Atheist

By Ronald Murphy

NEW FALCON PUBLICATIONS
LAS VEGAS, NEVADA, U.S.A.

Copyright © 2013 by Ronald Murphy

All rights reserved. No part of this book, in part or in whole, may be reproduced, transmitted, or utilized, in any form or by any means, electronic or mechanical, including photocopying, recording, or by any information storage and retrieval system, without permission in writing from the publisher, except for brief quotations in critical articles, books and reviews.

International Standard Book Number:
10: 1561845604
13:978-1561845606

First Edition 2013

The paper used in this publication meets the minimum requirements of the American National Standard for Permanence of Paper for Printed Library Materials Z39.48-1984

NEW FALCON PUBLICATIONS
9550 South Eastern Avenue • Suite 253
Las Vegas, NV 89123
www.newfalcon.com
email: info@newfalcon.com

Table of Contents

Table of Contents *continued*

PART ONE

Introduction to Religion

BACKGROUND

"You're the Devil!"

That was the last thing I heard before my friend of many years slammed the phone down in frustration. I shouldn't have been surprised. I have become accustomed to this reaction when compelled to explain my beliefs—or lack thereof.

OK, in the beginning, religion was never a tremendous focus in my household as it was with so many other black families in our neighborhood. We didn't attend church, read the Bible, and except for meals, we didn't pray. Even then, I don't think I ever really understood the meaning behind our prayers. You might think, "Why wasn't I persuaded to go to church at an early age so I could be taught the virtues of the Christian faith?" My parents were educators; my mother retired from the public school system as an assistant superintendent, and my father retired from an administrator's position at CUNY (City University of New York). Before my father passed away in 1996 and my mother in 2012, becoming my own person and making uninfluenced decisions about my life were very important to them. They also hoped their children would be allowed to guide their lives without any overwhelming childhood indoctrinations. Some might get the impression that my parents allowed us to run wild with no principles guiding our lives. This could not be further from the truth. They were far stricter than many of the parents on our block, utilizing an old school methodology when it came to parenting. They didn't believe in sparing the rod and were adamant about instilling strong moral values. In our predominantly white neighborhood, they made their expectations clear, and weren't concerned with what the parents down the street allowed their children to do. Like most adolescents, we were encouraged to recognize and perform to our potential, offer and reciprocate kindness, and make our own informed life decisions without blindly following the crowd. To my parents, this was the most important of all.

I grew up in the quiet town of Maplewood, New Jersey. The fact that we were one of only a few black families in this predominantly white area never meant much to me. It was not until I was older that I felt the reality of racism, when I began dating my white high school sweetheart that I realized I was viewed differently. When college rolled around, my parents wanted me to have the opportunity to immerse myself in African American culture, to get the "black experience" as they say. Until this point, I was in the minority in every environment and school I attended.

After much debate, and my mother's wish for her twin boys to travel together for protection, we set off to an HBC/U or Historically Black College or University in North Carolina. Once arriving in this strange community, it didn't take me long to figure out that the Southeast, religion, and the African American community were three peas in the same pod. Not a day went by where I was not told to "Have a blessed day," or a reference wasn't made to God being good. One of the things that took some getting used too was the continual prayer before every function. No matter the event, we were led in prayer—marching band rehearsal, sporting events, lectures, and of course meals. I guess it was assumed that every-one who attended this historical black college was a Christian.

It also didn't take long before I had my first run-in with the more intense Southern Christian culture. It happened during the first week of classes. While walking across campus during class transition, I noticed a well-dressed gentleman standing on the street corner. He held a black book in one hand and a bullhorn in the other. This was certainly an odd sight for a suburban New Jersey teen. As I approached the building where my next class was to be held, I decided to have a seat on a nearby bench so I could satisfy my overwhelming curiosity. After a few minutes, he began to speak, "Repent, Repent! If you were to die today where would your soul spend eternity? Sinners repent!"

He went on for several minutes, mesmerizing me. Astonished by his bold approach, I stared in his direction in an almost trance-like state, engrossed by his every word. I had never seen anyone preach in such an animated fashion before, no less on a public sidewalk. After a while, my expression of amazement turned to one of concern. Everyone was ignoring him! And they weren't just purposely avoiding his path; he seemed almost invisible to the entire student body. My focus quickly shifted from the en-thusiastic speaker to the hordes of passing students taking no notice of our lively guest. I tried to find someone who would at least acknowledge his presence. For my own peace of mind, I needed to be sure this experience was not like a bad episode of *The Twilight Zone*. You know, where I would be the only one that could see him. Maybe the mystery meat in the cafeteria was catch-ing up with me. Out of sheer frustration, I stopped a passerby, pointed to the speaker still condemning the masses, and timidly asked, "Can you see him?"

She looked at me oddly, and said, "He's here all the time. Where are you from?"

I told her, and explained that I had never seen anything like it. She laughed and said, "Well you're in the Bible belt now, so get used to it."

With a surprised look on my face, I asked, "What's the Bible belt?"

She laughed again and said, "You can't be that naïve," and then walked off. But I really didn't know what she was talking about.

By this time, the zealous speaker had laid down his megaphone and began passing out a small pamphlet. Again, the irresistible pull of curiosity had me in its grip. What was he handing out? Unfortunately, his message appeared to fall on deaf ears because it seemed like everyone was refusing his gift. I decided I was going to wait until everyone had moved on to class before grabbing a copy for myself.

While sitting in the back of my music theory class, I read through this small piece of literature and was completely surprised by its conspicuous message. In an unapologetic, gloves-off style, it exclaimed that the world would be coming to an end in our lifetime, and that Jesus Christ, our Lord and Savior, would be returning to judge all mankind. If you were found worthy, you would spend the afterlife in God's perfect kingdom. But if you were found unworthy, you would be doomed to spend eternity in a fiery hell!

This fascinated me. With all my freshman naiveté intact, and no real knowledge of religion, I embraced this notion. I had no idea that everything was so final after you died. After class, I bolted across campus tightly clutching the catalyst for my newly forming ideas. With great anticipation, I headed to the dorm room of my new collegiate friend, Valerie, hoping she could shed some light on my obvious ignorance. I also wanted to see her; I held a bit of a schoolboy crush on this small-town girl who I'd come to affectionately call "Little One." She stood four feet eleven inches and was the epitome of a black southern belle. I hastily explained what happened, and she shook her head and said, "That's not the way to bring people to the Lord."

I quickly explained that I didn't know anything about the subject and needed her to start from the beginning. She laughed and said, "They don't have churches in New Jersey?"

"Of course they do," I replied, "but since my family and I did not attend weekly services, I am a bit in the dark about religion."

This is when my informal education began. She prefaced our conversation with the assertion that religion is a personal experience and can vary widely depending on your audience. While it might seem like I was frantically immersing myself in religion after such a brief experience, I was simply satisfying a strong curiosity about this socially pervasive construct completely foreign to me. In high school, I was a bit of a nerd and really struggled to make friends and develop relationships with peers from my own race. I'm sure this became one of the many reasons why my parents thought I needed to be more involved with my own culture and heritage by attending a historically black college. Now I was living amongst the very individuals that had shunned me during my high school years. If religion was the dominant social mechanism in play in this Southern black society, then I was going to learn enough not only to survive, but also to excel.

During my college career, I was just a casual religious observer, rarely participating in church services. I followed this faith-based ideology because I saw it as a relaxed way of fitting in. While I eventually prayed over more than just my food, and began to incorporate the habit-forming thought processes at the core of all religions (I will address this more deeply later), I was not a strict observer of religious ceremony and belief. Although I can say that over my collegiate years, belief in God became second nature to me. Today I can also say I reached this certainty through some kind of communal osmosis, in which the prevailing notion of God was an absolute certainty among the people with whom I interacted daily. This concept gradually infiltrated my psyche, and was something I learned to believe without question. To me God existed, and always had!

Moving to Atlanta

Let's fast-forward nearly a decade, to my move to Atlanta, where I have since settled. Before I even unpacked my bags, I was indoctrinated into the highly religious climate of Georgia. While walking through Lenox Mall, I was approached by a gentlemen appearing to be lost. I quickly explained that I was new to the city and barely able to find my way to the mall. He immediately struck up a friendly conversation, interacting with me as though we'd been close friends for many years. We chatted for a while before I told him that I needed to go. As soon as I tried to step away, he unexpectedly, and somewhat excitedly, asked if I would be willing to join him for Bible study. His change in demeanor suggested that this was the only reason he stopped to talk with me in the first place.

"No, thank you," I quickly replied.

It wasn't because I didn't have an interest in studying the Bible, but it was more about my apprehension about visiting a stranger's home in an unfamiliar new city.

He grew visibly frustrated, and asked if I would at least be willing to visit his church on Sunday morning. His tone suggested I owed him that much. Reluctantly, I gave him my number and told him to call me with the pertinent information, and I might be willing to check it out.

I would later regret this decision.

As the week wore on, I received several calls from my new-found religious friend. Each seemed to be more anxious than the last, as if by refusing his invitation I would be injuring him. With a deep lack of enthusiasm, I decided to return his call to explain that I would attend the upcoming Sunday service. Hopefully, this would satisfy his almost stalker-like behavior.

As I walked onto church grounds, I noticed my spiritual sponsor standing among several other members. He eagerly motioned for me to join them. As I approached, he turned to the small group and said, "This is the guy I was telling you about." Now I felt real apprehension about visiting this church. I thought to myself, *we only spoke for a few minutes in a crowded mall. What could you have possibly learned about me in that short period of time that would be worth sharing with others?*

Almost instantly, they began to question me about where I was from, what part of town did I stay in, what church did I attend in New Jersey, and could they have my phone number? I avoided the probing questions by claiming I needed to use the restroom. While staring at my reflection in the bathroom mirror, I thought, *what in the hell did I get myself into?* I stayed there awhile before someone came in after me. I pretended like I was finishing up and exited the bathroom.

When we entered the main sanctuary, it became very apparent to everyone that I was a newcomer. I was escorted to the front row, where they invited me to sit down with the other "Guests." I use the term loosely because, by the looks on their faces, it was obvious to me they had made the same mistake I did by accepting a seemingly innocent invitation. A few minutes later, the choir began singing as the pastor was led to the stage by his faithful followers. After a short praise and prayer session, the collection plate was passed around. While much of the congregation's behavior seemed atypical, there was an obvious seriousness attached to the amount of money that would be collected for the Lord. The preacher even told the congregation that God would block blessings for those who refused to give back to his kingdom. This sentiment permeated the church, and was never more evident than when I passed the offering basket to the next person in the aisle without making the expected donation. The old adage, "If looks could kill" certainly held new meaning for me.

After the offering, the old school pastor began to preach the word of God. He started quietly at first, quoting scripture from a few random places in the Bible, before ramping up into an agitated state. He frequently singled out those of us in the front row as the new disciples of the faith, and explained to his faithful flock we needed to be led in the ways of the Lord. He would often jump around and run across the stage, acting out every simplistic point he was trying to make. I thought to myself: *I get it; you don't need an analogy for every easily understood idea.*

As I looked around the main sanctuary, I saw a disturbing trance-like, devotional stare coming from many of the members. It felt almost dangerous to me. While in North Carolina, I very rarely attended church, only visiting a few dozen times during my entire collegiate career. Those people were rigidly sterile compared to this theatrical presentation that I was now witnessing.

During the height of the sermon, the preacher approached our group of visibly apprehensive newcomers. After asking us to rise to our feet, he paced back and forth in front of our line, as if he were an evil prison warden trying to figure out which detainee to make an example of. Just my luck, he chose me. He placed his hand on my head and began to mumble in my direction. Apparently, my reaction was insufficient, because he began to shake me lightly at first, and then more violently as his unrecognizable ramblings became louder. Simply wanting the shaking to stop, I cried out and raised my hands, assuming the congregation and preacher would be looking for some type of reaction from me. With a cocky reassurance, he proudly announced, "The Holy Spirit is certainly dwelling in the house of the Lord today, and it has some work to do."

With my eyes closed, I slumped back into my seat. I could tell his words had incensed the crowd because the shouting reached a furious climax.

After the pastor made his way back to the podium, I slowly staggered to my feet and made my way to the back of the church. I told an usher, who seemed to be guarding the door like a centurion, that I needed to use the restroom to take some medicine. The usher reluctantly allowed me out of the main sanctuary and kept the door propped open to ensure that I was only heading to the restroom. As soon as his back was turned, I made a beeline to the side door, running to my car and speeding off church grounds. Later that night, several of that saintly squad left some rather rude messages on my voicemail: "You're just the Devil in disguise." And, "God will seek vengeance on your kind." These were just a few of the messages that I ended up deleting.

I quickly realized this was not the church I was being called to! That's an understatement; I thought they were a crazy cult. I knew I would have to be far more careful in the future. While I had not attended church in quite some time, I certainly wanted to look for a spiritual home in this new city. Even with my limited exposure to Christianity, I knew that I was not supposed to be in a new location for very long without finding a church home, so I could continue fellowship with other Christians and maintain the divine covering over my life.

After telling a trusted friend about my experience, she quickly asked me what kind of churches I attended as a child. I explained that organized religion was not a major focus in my household, and that I did not attend church in New Jersey. In the same breath, I assured my friend that morality and the distinction between right and wrong were strictly taught and enforced. I went on to admit that I also hadn't attended church much in North Carolina. When asked why, I explained that I just didn't understand the idea of an all-powerful God who dwelled in the heavens, and made man in his own image, etc., so I never really gave it a chance. She laughed and said, "You must have faith. Faith that God will direct you to the right church and guide you to your divine destiny, so you can fulfill the calling that He has ordained for your life."

After my unsettling encounter with that fanatical congregation, I grew very apprehensive about what churches I would attend. However, I knew that I needed a spiritual home, and so the search began.

GIVING MYSELF TO CHRIST

Within a few months of my brush with the cult, I was introduced to one of the largest and most popular churches in Atlanta.
I really enjoyed the services and it seemed to be a good fit for
my learning style. The pastor simply spoke to the congregation
without the ornate showmanship that I had witnessed at many of
the other churches I had visited. After only attending services for
a few months, I casually asked a few of the elders what I needed
to do in order to gain support and favor from my heavenly father. I received answers like: "study the word," "live a Christ-like
existence," "allow the common man to see God's glory in your
actions." But most importantly, "get involved in ministries so you
can spread the gospel to others."

I took that advice. I joined the church orchestra, attended service every Sunday, became a regular fixture at Bible studies, and
worked diligently to change my lifestyle. I wanted to really give
Christianity the proverbial college try! I didn't drink, smoke, curse
much or have tons of sex, but I did change the people with whom
I associated. I was told to only have close associations with true
believers. My friends or acquaintances had to believe as I did, or
they had to go. While it was difficult, I simply saw it as a necessary step for me to grow closer to God. For most people, this meant

I could simply back off slowly, and fade-to-black if you will. Unfortunately for others, I had to sit them down and have a heart to heart conversation, explaining that they should come to Christ. I felt my newfound life was on a sort of autopilot. I was attending services, involved in ministries, and living without a spiritual care in the world.

While in church, I was amazed at how much everyone accepted me. Church members would practically jump over pews just to say good morning. I was attending one of the largest black churches in Atlanta, and every time I sat in the pews, I saw a different face, each willing to talk with me. This reaction stood in stark contrast from the one I would receive while walking local malls and interacting with everyday Atlanta residents. The personable approach of the churchgoers became a huge draw for me. I could make new friends much faster in church than anywhere else. Often, church members would invite me to their homes for Bible study without even knowing me. It was also a place where you could be accepted regardless of who you were, what you looked like, or how much money you had. The familiarity and camaraderie that normally took weeks or months to build in other environments seemed to only take days in church. I instantly thought to myself, if I was a lonely person and craved basic human companionship, this is the place I needed to be. Church was the one place that would be socially consistent. I would be able to see the same type of people from week to week, in a captive environment where everyone is expected to be friendly, inviting, and dare I say, Christ-like. The normally bad attitudes to which I was exposed in the secular world seemed to be non-existent in the church.

It was a long time before I realized that the persona church members held during service was not the same one they carried into the outside world.

Everything was completely new to me. I felt like a child learning life all over again. It reminded me of my naiveté while in college. There was so much I had never seen nor been aware of, and it always seemed like I was the only one that didn't get the memo.

At one of the first services I attended, I showed how little I knew about my faith, more specifically, this new church. One morning I couldn't sleep, so I decided to attend the 6 a.m. service with a friend. I was told that only the most devout members attended this early morning congregation. Early in the service, while the choir was singing, a woman started running around the church, gyrating before falling to the floor. She began to mumble, but I couldn't understand any of her uttered gibberish. I was horrified! I thought she was having a seizure. I was in the middle of the pew and couldn't get to her, so I frantically motioned it to the usher at the end of the aisle. My neighbor, who had invited me to this service, told me to calm down, all the while overlooking the woman convulsing a few yards away.

Ignoring my friend, I continued to point out the woman in distress. To my surprise, the usher calmly walked over to her and held her skirt down. I couldn't understand what was going on. This woman obviously needed medical attention, and yet everyone around me was choosing to ignore her, acting like it was no big deal. The usher seemed more concerned about keeping her skirt down than her well-being. A few minutes later, after the music subsided, so did her reaction. She was helped to her feet and back to her seat. Exhausted, she collapsed into the pew, and appeared to be in a euphoric daze. While I had witnessed all kinds of reactions during church service, I had never seen anything like this. Once the congregation was seated, I tapped my neighbor, and asked her what happened. With a slight smile on her face, she said, "You're newer to this than I thought."

Suddenly, I felt really embarrassed. "Yeah, I guess I didn't get the memo," I said.

With a doubtful look, she went on to say, "She supposedly caught the holy ghost."

"What! What's the Holy Ghost? Is that like the Holy Spirit?" I replied.

Her frown turned to a smile. "Yeah, It's when the Holy Spirit or the supernatural presence of God inhabits your body. You become overwhelmed by the energy and often speak in the old language or tongues."

Since I didn't want to seem like a total idiot, I nodded in agreement and left well enough alone. Later that night, I sat in my bed wondering at what point in my walk the Holy Ghost would possess me. While I was amazed by this experience and definitely wanted to get closer to God, I wasn't so sure about the idea of being possessed by a supernatural presence if it was going to make me act like that.

Embracing the Belief

After attending services for about a year, I began to pose some of the questions that had kept me from attending church more frequently in North Carolina. They initially went unasked because I wanted to find a church home where I felt a sense of family. Cultivating meaningful and personal relationships was my first priority, followed by making inquiries about my faith. I wanted to be able to ask questions without the fear of being judged or ridiculed simply because I didn't know as much as my Christian neighbor. Unfortunately, I heard the same generic answers I received in North Carolina, "Just have faith." While in this case, people responded to me in a very loving and sincere manner, I didn't understand why the use of this vague term was considered such a comprehensive answer, and so absolute.

Faith is the foundation of every religion, and arguably one of the most important words used in all religious culture. The dictionary defines faith as: *"Belief and trust in, and loyalty to God. A firm belief in something for which there is no proof or evidence, complete trust in something that is believed especially with strong conviction."*

Faith was certainly my biggest enemy in my search for answers. Every time I asked a pertinent question that others perceived as probing, they threw up the all-encompassing heavenly
shield of faith. This is why I wasn't more involved in religious services in North Carolina. From my perspective, my questions were
reasonable. Since the religions of the world have vastly different
beliefs and deities, what evidence existed for not only a supreme
being, but also our specific God? Why wouldn't God perform the
amazing miracles, documented throughout the Bible, in modern
day times? Seemed to me it would go a long way toward providing the evidence and verification so many people seek or require.
Since Jesus was a humble carpenter and, by all accounts, led a
relatively meager life, why did so many church leaders seem to
lead such lavish lifestyles? These were just a handful of the initial
questions with which I wrestled as I began my walk.

Unfortunately, every time I spoke with someone about my
questions, I was told to have faith. But I was searching for a suit-
able reason to have faith. So, I wondered, is faith a reasonable
reason to ignore...well, reason? In my first attempt to resolve this
conundrum, I began to search for similar examples of extreme
faith throughout our society. By doing this, I was hoping to gain a
greater understanding why faith was so important.

It didn't take long for me to realize there were NO comparable
examples. I couldn't find anything in our society unsupported by
evidence that was taken at face value, and was believed through
blind faith. Most importantly, I saw very few social constructs
where it was considered so appalling to merely question the validity of the system, or search for answers. Many people with whom
I spoke maintained that we have faith in almost everything in our
lives. They cited marriage, science, and even the sun rising each
day as comparable examples of equivalent religious faith. I had
to point out that none of those examples were relevant to the

comparison I was trying to make. For me, there were significant differences between blind religious faith, and faith in the every-day occurrences listed above. While explaining my position, three words immediately came to mind: consistency, predictability, and testability! We have faith in our marriages, because trust grows over an extended period of time, and a pattern of predictable consistent behavior from our companion is established—sometimes tested by hardship or conflict. We have faith in science because of the predictability from its testable observations, resulting technology or advancements. If I doubt the findings, or even the science, I can recreate the experiments and examine all the evidence that pointed to the original theory.

Needless to say, I had my doubts about faith. More importantly, I was trying to figure out why any attempt to validate aspects of religious belief was considered so sinful and forbidden, carrying a trip to hell as punishment. This quickly raised more questions. Since the holy book is considered the Word of God, and He and his Word are considered perfect, why was it prohibited to ask questions? Why were those who asked questions shunned? Couldn't the religion and doctrine of the most powerful and perfect being in the Universe stand up to the mildest of human scrutiny? The only reason I wanted answers was because I was still holding onto the idealistic notion that I would not only be saving souls for Christ by showing them His glory, but also convincing and converting the masses seduced by false religions. Many years later, I remember hearing Matt Dilihaunty, a host of the popular show *Atheist Experience*, mention to a caller that during his religious walk, he was always trying to satisfy the requirement of the biblical scripture in I Peter 3:15: *"But in your hearts revere Christ as Lord. Always be prepared to give an answer to everyone who asks you to give the reason for the hope that you have, but do this with gentleness and respect."*

This was the same sentiment I held when I began my search for answers. I just wanted to know my beliefs were true and that I could intelligently explain them to others. So I began to suspect that many of my fellow church members were simply not knowledgeable enough to answer my questions. So I pushed forward in my religious walk without answers, setting them aside until I had an opportunity to speak with someone far more knowledgeable than the average churchgoer.

In retrospect, this might seem like a really foolish decision, but I was not raised in the church. I wanted to receive all the blessings associated with faith. The heartfelt testimonies of people who say God touched their lives were incredibly alluring. I saw this as an amazing relief, since I was going through some challenges myself. All I had to do was seek the kingdom of God with all my heart and the rest would be bestowed onto me. I wanted divine favor and an omnipotent being on my side.

Initially, it was very liberating to let go of the questions and operate on faith. It allowed me to genuinely give Christianity an honest shot. By allowing myself to "let go, and let God," as they say, I was able to fully explore my faith without the need to over-analyze each encounter. My spiritual education progressed and my walk with the Lord deepened. While the unanswered questions about my faith still lay dormant, I felt by giving myself over to God that he would effortlessly provide me answers in a way no earthly man could. So I pressed forward, looking for every opportunity to intensify my spiritual experiences. I was often awestruck at the love and favor I felt God was showing my life, and how quickly our relationship grew. I felt happy when I thought about God and deepening my walk with him. While I didn't know as much as my neighbor and hadn't been in pursuit of His grace as long as the church elders, I felt just as connected to God as anyone else. I felt a sense of power, an attitude that I could conquer all, and a future calling in the ministry. I wasn't sure in what capacity I would be aiding the kingdom, but I felt a yearning to be involved.

There was one particular experience that really shaped this desire and solidified my perception that ministry would be a part of my future. One Halloween night, a friend of mine from a neighboring church invited me to something called a "Revelation Hay Ride." Here's how it worked. A tractor pulled several wagons full of hay. Guests sat atop the bales while being pulled to prearranged stops on the elaborate course. Each stop was another interpreted scene from the book of Revelation. The re-enactment was very powerful and detailed. While there were many stops on this virtual tour of the end times, the first scene held the most impact for me. As our convoy came to a standstill, I saw an elaborate set depicting a highway scene in which cars were piled up from what appeared to be the result of multiple car accidents. In the seats of several vehicles, clothes sat perfectly positioned, as if the bodies had simply dematerialized, whisked away by some unseen force. I knew before the narrator spoke that only the hand of a loving God would be so kind as to save his anointed children from such hardship. The narrator told us that God would be pulling believers to heaven before the seven years of trials and tribulations began here on earth. This event would be called the rapture, and would culminate in the shedding of our corporeal forms and our souls ascending to heaven. I was excited. I remember feeling very privileged, as though I had a secret bunker that only the chosen few knew about. No matter how bad things on earth became, I would be safe.

The speaker went on to say some of the faithful would be left behind to do God's work. That He would require foot soldiers to show the masses of nonbelievers God's glory. As soon as he finished his sentence, I felt an overwhelming wave of emotion and feelings, which I quickly associated with the divine. I instantly made a connection to God, and honestly believed that this would be one of my life callings. After the great rapture, I would be helping people make this difficult transition to the one true God. I actually *wanted* to be left behind (like the book series) so I could save souls for the Lord. I prayed a quick prayer: "God, if this is your calling for my life, I accept it graciously and humbly. I ask that you prepare me for this task, so I may do it justice. As always, I will follow your Will where ever it may lead me. It's in the holy name of Jesus that I pray, Amen."

The next scene on our tour quickly interrupted my impromptu prayer. The post-apocalyptic landscape showed a family approaching a small compound with a cross affixed to the main gate. Our narrator told us that a year had passed since the great rapture, and the human population had dropped from seven billion to several hundred million scattered around the globe. The featured family had been wandering across the countryside for weeks, trying to find an encampment of survivors they could join. They knew they wouldn't be able to survive much longer without help. As they approached the gate, the unmistakable sound of chambered shotgun shells broke the calm of the night. A spotlight bright enough to turn night into day enveloped the weary family and froze them in their tracks. Within a few seconds, they heard a voice from inside the compound say, "Stop right there, none but believers may enter our sanctuary."

The father and self appointed leader of the family replied, "I have a wife and two children. We have come a long way. Please let us in."

His plea was quickly met with, "Are you believers, my son?"

The father paused. While he, his wife and son were believers, he knew his daughter had never accepted the faith. Before the father could even respond, his daughter bellowed, "We are people, and it shouldn't matter if we believe in your particular faith!"

Visibly upset, the father told her to be silent. Unfortunately, the damage was done. As quickly as the daughter made her declaration, an ultimatum came from the faceless voice: "Only believers in our Lord Jesus Christ may grace our land. So go away from here non-believer, only the faithful may enter here."

The narrator told us that the daughter had been seduced by false religions and beliefs, never accepting Christ as the one true God. With a deliberate importance, he explained that after the rapture there would be no tolerance for following a false God. He quickly reminded the group that God's first commandment stated not to worship any other Gods but him. He added that there would still be doubters in the future, and tough choices would have to be made.

"Whom you align yourself with could make all the difference in where your soul spends eternity," he said.

The scene picked up. The father was now forced to make a very difficult decision. Either he would split the family apart and accept the much-needed help from this overtly Christian community, leaving his un-accepting daughter behind, or keep the family together and look somewhere else for their much needed food and shelter. The scene was very tense and silent as everyone awaited his response. The father stared at his daughter for what seemed like an eternity before he turned his back to her and said, "Go away from here, you are not a child of God, and so you are no child of mine."

I remember thinking how stupid she was. What would it take to convince this deluded girl that she needed to get right with God, especially after the events of the rapture? Clearly that act, chronicled in the Holy Bible, would have demonstrated who the true God was!

Later that night, while lying awake in bed, I wondered if I would have been able to make such a difficult decision. Would

I be able to hear God's voice so clearly as to always walk in his desired path, no matter how much hardship I would be forced to endure? -

That became one of the goals I set for myself: to hear from God directly. I wanted to be as bountifully anointed as my pastors and spiritual leaders, who seemed to have an unmatched kinship with God. During service, I was always amazed at how "on time" each message appeared to be. My pastor always seemed to speak to my circumstances. This uncanny ability really gave credence to his power and connection to our heavenly father. I knew having God speak to me would symbolize a true connection, and represent a new level of faith in my life. But I also knew I was still considered an unclean vessel because I had not given myself to Christ.

Late one Sunday afternoon, I could no longer ignore the relentless pull from God. I decided to give myself to the Lord. Toward the end of service, the pastor made the altar call. I left my pew and headed up front to thunderous applause. I was doing the right thing. I knew it. I felt it. After service was dismissed, all of the new disciples and I were taken to a smaller room where we were led in a prayer to give ourselves to Christ. After the prayer, I didn't feel any different, but I expected that to change as I began my walk.

The following Sunday, I was baptized at the church and scheduled into new members classes.

New Member's Classes

I entered the class for new members with obvious anticipation. I was so excited about taking my first steps in this proclaimed new life. As class started, the instructor eagerly quoted scripture before she even told us her name. I felt instantly overwhelmed, thinking, *Wow, I'm so far behind everyone else who was introduced to Christ at an early age, I hope I don't embarrass myself.*

On the first day of class we simply introduced ourselves to each other, and the instructor assigned us basic reading. Later that evening, while trying to study these scriptural assignments, those dormant unanswered questions resurfaced with an almost purposeful vengeance. I figured they would be seen as foolish if posed in the classroom setting, largely because I still held the persistent belief that it was my inexperience with the Bible, its scriptures, stories and ideology, that kept me from finding answers. Nevertheless, I knew the first duty of any saved Christian was to bring others into the fold. I needed readily available answers for the non-believers to whom I would be ministering. So once and for all, I had to find answers for these persistently invasive questions about my faith.

During the next class, our instructor outlined some of the topics we would cover during the next several weeks. She immediately informed us that our high school biology lessons presented
incorrect information about the origins of life. She explained that
God created the heavens and the earth, as well as man in his own
image. All my classmates nodded in agreement, as if this were
purely review. On the other hand, I was a little bothered, wanting
to know why I wasted time in science classes being taught incorrect information. "Why wasn't this information taught in high
school?" I hastily asked. She explained that schools were forced
to teach science and give no thought to the supernatural. She went
on to tell us the story of Adam and Eve, as well as the long lineage
of their divine offspring. I was fascinated, and remember making
the comment, "So we are all related?"

She looked at me rather confused. I clarified my statement
by saying; "If you were to trace the lineage of anyone back far
enough, you will eventually get to Adam and Eve."

She nodded in agreement and kept teaching. Later, while
reading from the Bible, I asked, "How was this book written?"
With fullest confidence and assurance, she at first said it was written by God, and then restated that the Holy Spirit inhabited devout
believers and Jesus's disciples, and they wrote the book. I then
asked, "So how can I prove our God's existence to others, without
using a book that was written by man?"

She said, "God is invisible and can't be perceived by the
earthly sciences or our normal human senses."

I then muttered, "I don't understand why other religions exist
and why God allows them to flourish. I have been told time and
time again that he is a jealous God, and the worship of a false deity is one of the greatest sins imaginable. So why doesn't He just
get rid of them?"

At this point, she became annoyed with me. Her tone changed
from gentle mentor to authoritarian. "Are you sure you made the
right decision?"

Her question bewildered me. "What decision?" I replied.

"The one you made to Jesus Christ, the one to be saved!"

I was shocked she would ask me such a question in front of the entire class. Still, I respectfully replied, "Yes, of course, but I don't want to be an ignorant Christian who simply spouts information I was taught, especially when the validity of which is not apparent. If I'm going to base my entire life off these beliefs, it's very important to me to fully understand them, and know they are correct."

"You can't question God; it's a sin!" she replied.

By now, everyone in the class was angrily staring at me, as if to say, "Shut up you idiot. You don't know what you're talking about."

"Just study the word, have faith, and the answers you're searching for will come in time," my instructor said.

I was so embarrassed! I felt like a troublemaker, when that was never my intention. I managed to alienate myself from my instructor and fellow classmates in one fell swoop. Way to go, Ron!

For the remainder of the lesson, I sat quietly and took notes. I didn't have any issues in taking aspects of Christianity on faith, but it seemed really irresponsible not to confirm or get answers for the most fundamental questions. Especially when I was going to base my entire earthly existence on this doctrine.

Later that night, my embarrassment turned to anger. I paced in my apartment, upset and frustrated. I couldn't understand why my simple questions weren't answered so we could have all moved on with the lesson. I only wanted to build a strong factual foundation to support my spiritual journey. I decided I wasn't going any further with the classes until I received satisfactory answers to my longstanding questions.

PART TWO:

Why I left the Church

EMERGING DOUBT:
THE SEARCH FOR EVIDENCE

After withdrawing from the new member classes, I continued attending church, hoping I would find my answers outside of a formal classroom. Over the next several months I began to systematically search for opportunities to ask questions in a more relaxed setting, where I could enter into a casual conversation and collect my much-needed answers without being perceived as the class agitator. I quickly realized that every time I made an inquiry, not only did I run into a religious brick wall, but I also seemed to upset many by even mentioning certain subjects. The only answers I ever received were the ones I had been hearing for years: "Just have faith," "You can't question God," "It just is," "Where do you think we came from if not from God?" The list goes on.

At this point, I became a closet skeptic.

I was done asking questions and drawing crazy looks. I knew I was going to have to find answers on my own. Unfortunately, the more research I conducted, the more questions I had. Now I began to scrutinize the church service itself. I found myself questioning everything about the experience. I realized that the words that seemed just for me, were generic terms that would apply to anyone. For example, our pastor would say things like, "I know many of you are going through something out there, but I'm here to tell you that God is going to lift that burden."

While this declaration was met with thunderous applause, it seemed rather vague and way too generic to be a credible test of a proclaimed prophet. Of course, we are all going through something in our lives. At the same time, if anyone inspected their lives closely enough, they would realize they were resolving issues as well. I likened the experience to a phony psychic who makes very vague predictions that, when examined closely enough, can be associated with something going on in our everyday lives.

My favorite part of the week was always the end of Wednesday night Bible study. This was the time for everyone to give testimonies about how God had touched their lives. These examples of God's will in action were always promoted as the greatest evidence for his awesome power. I remember three particular stories that caught my attention, stories that I initially took at face value years ago, but now prompted me to ask some pertinent follow-up questions.

Story 1: A young woman stood up and explained that her grandfather had been diagnosed with cancer. His doctors said the outlook was not good. While she adamantly prayed for his recovery, she reluctantly started planning for the worse and began making funeral arrangements and putting his affairs in order. One night, her grandfather was very restless and couldn't sleep. The next morning, while having his regular check up, the doctors were astonished to find no sign of the cancer. He had endured painful treatments for several months, and was growing more and more depressed. She went on to explain that she believed God heard her prayers and saved her grandfather's life. She also testified that God wouldn't put any more on you than you can bear.

After Bible study I approached the woman and asked, "How long was he in treatments?"

She replied, "About ten months."

"What caused the cancer?"

"The doctors aren't sure."

She went on to say her grandfather was getting more involved in his church and may have angered the Devil, so it was probably his plan to take her grandfather's life so he couldn't do the Lord's work.

About a year later, I saw the woman again and asked her how her grandfather was doing. She broke down in tears and explained that he had passed away a few weeks before. The cancer returned and grew uncontrollably, until it finally took his life. I offered my condolences and said, "He's in God's kingdom now." I did not know what else to say, but it sure put a smile on her face.

I remembered how she initially claimed that the Devil was trying to kill her father. However, scripture says that only God has dominion over the saved and the faithful. She testified that God cured him, but I wanted to know why He would have inflicted the man with cancer to begin with? Why was God being credited for the cure when her grandfather received chemotherapy for ten-months? Especially when the cancer simply went into remission and was not eradicated? Of course, I never posed these questions to her, but I felt odd being the only one to look at this experience from an objective viewpoint.

Story 2: A tearful woman slowly stood up and warned the other female members in the group, "God has asked us not to fornicate." She quoted a scripture I can't remember, and added, "You don't want the wrath of Gods upon you."

She went on to explain how she had been dating a guy who she knew was unsavory, and that God had been sending her clear signs that he was a bad influence and unfaithful. She often found phone numbers in his pockets, and random women would call all hours of the night, rudely hanging up when they heard her voice. Some nights, he wouldn't even bother coming home. He never provided any explanations for his whereabouts, claiming she was just a jealous nag. Unfortunately, she continued to sleep with him. She explained that God was trying to tell her to end this relationship, but she wouldn't listen. One day, while getting her normal check-up, her gynecologist called her into the office and told her she had herpes. She was devastated, and immediately called her unfaithful boyfriend and told him it was over.

With a motherly look, she gazed over the crowd of mostly women and said, "When God is sending you signs, you need to listen, because He might just be trying to save you from something. If I had listened, I would not have this incurable disease."

I felt sorry for her, but I now could not help wondering why God would send hints. Why not appear before this woman and tell her to leave her trifling boyfriend? Or simply influence this bad boy to move on? Why would God hand down such an incurable punishment for doing something many of the unmarried church members were guilty of? She was certainly not the only person having premarital sex.

Story 3: A gentleman stood up at the end of the service and told the group his life story. "I have stolen some things, robbed a few stores, and been involved in several acts that I am not proud of," he said. "But I hit a low point when I was strung out on crack. I'm here to tell you that only God could have gotten me off that pipe! I tried quitting several times, with no luck. It wasn't until Jesus came into my life that I had the supernatural strength to get clean."

While this story was compelling, I made it a point to speak with him after service. He explained that he had never been in a formal treatment program until after he had entered the church, and that they offered to provide him food and shelter as long as he continued to attend services and was enrolled in the drug rehabilitation program.

I took it all in, but the big question billowing in my mind was: If he had never tried a formal program before, and the church was unconsciously bribing the gentleman by offering him a place to stay and daily meals as long as he continued to come to services and rehab classes, why should we believe his getting clean was a supernatural event?

At this point, I began to realize that unless these personal testaments could meet some exacting criteria, how could they been seen as reliable proof of Godly intervention. Without that, everything and anything that happened to someone could be construed and manipulated to be an act of God. If God is perfect and all-powerful, why would he need any help performing miracles, or demonstrating his deliberate will? Why would the most powerful being in the Universe consistently perform tasks that could be misinterpreted as random chance, or the work of men?

I understand that many people don't believe in chance and claim that it doesn't exist, but that's simply not true. People believe in luck, good or bad, depending on the circumstances. Chance is defined as: *"The absence of any cause of events that can be predicted, understood, or controlled: often personalized or treated as a positive agency."* It happens randomly and cannot be predicted.

In every testimony I heard, the believer alleged that God's judgment was a direct result of their faith or disobedience to his will, and I was willing to believe these claims if they had been followed by verifiable evidence. Many will say, it was true to them and that's all that matters. But why should anyone else be persuaded by these testimonies? How can personal interpretations provide a reliable method for discerning truth? I imagine that many of the people that believe the validity of these personal truths would not be as open to accepting them if they ran against the grain of their long-standing beliefs. I wonder if they would maintain that personal experiences were reliable if someone were to assert that another God was the only true deity?

I would think that the faithful believer would be very apprehensive about claiming God was involved in something without any verification, simply because they could be attaching a deed to their God that He never truly endorsed. I would be more apt to believe the claims of Godly intervention if these alleged miracles were required to meet some type of criteria. For instance, if everyone who didn't share the faith in question, never received these God-like blessings, and there was a consistent pattern to the dispersal, this would begin to prove your case. Unfortunately, when I critically examined the scenarios, everything credited to the Christian God was neither consistent nor unique to the faith. I began to take notes every time I heard a testimony. On every occasion when I applied simple logic or reason, the claim didn't seem like the product of an all-powerful God.

At this point, I took a step back to reexamine the whole idea of religion. After watching a related video on the net, I had to sincerely and definitively ask myself: *Does it matter to me if my beliefs are true or just feel true to me, and are comfortable?* The sobering answer: I wanted the truth, no matter how unsettling it might be, and so my beliefs most assuredly needed to be as true as possible, not just comforting. That being said, I began my quest for definitive answers from the beginning of my religious walk.

EXPLORING THE BIBLE

When I first began to question my belief system, I remember having a conversation with a non-believer. He claimed the only reason I believed in God was because it was taught to me as a child. Confidently, I mentioned to him that I did not grow up in the church, and that he was completely wrong. With a look of disbelief, he asked, "Then why do you believe in God?"

I told him I had faith, and the Bible tells me God is real. Even though I had my own doubts about my faith, I was too prideful to let any of those sentiments leak out in this conversation.

My counterpart asked, "So…how was the Bible created? How do you know it's true?"

The question caught me off guard, because I really didn't have a firm understanding of the Bible's origins. It was never explained in new member's classes or church services. After a long pause, which underscored my inability to answer his question, he said, "If you don't know its beginnings, how can you know it's the word of God?"

How *was* the Bible created? Initially I'd been content to simply believe that God wrote it through the hand of man. It had been something I just blindly accepted without ever feeling it needed verification. But now I knew I was going to need answers to move forward. Before beginning my investigation, I felt very apprehensive, even scared! I wasn't sure if I was going to be okay with the answers I might find. While a skeptic, I always held onto the idea that I would run into someone or some piece of information that would flawlessly answer all my questions, allowing me to rededicate myself to the faith. So I had to ask myself, did I really want to open Pandora's box?

I quickly realized that the entire Judeo-Christian beliefs and culture are based on the Bible's scriptures and stories. Without them, there would be little to no accounts of Jesus, His miracles, dying for our sins, resurrection, etc. So yes, I did need to know its origins! But what if I didn't find the answers that supported my already wavering faith? Would I be able to continue to accept it as a divinely inspired doctrine?

This anxiety consumed me. It was akin to the dread people sometimes feel about going to the doctor's office, the fear of being told something they didn't want to hear, something that has the potential to change their life forever.

Nevertheless, after a little soul-searching, I started my research. I quickly realized it was not going to be easy. In fact, it was the most convoluted information I've ever looked up. I wanted unbiased facts about the origin of the Bible, verifiable through multiple sources. Unfortunately, this proved to be very difficult. After reading through quite a bit of material, I was surprised at how many different perspectives and interpretations existed. Depending on the site, article, or book, the reader was left with a different spin on the validity and accuracy of the text. Some information would say things like, "The consistency of the Bible was impressive and extremely reliable, painstakingly passed down through the ages by direct descendants of eyewitnesses that had first hand information." Others would write, "The Bible is completely unreliable, a jumble of conflicting ideas borrowed from earlier works written from multiple perspectives, that can't be verified, with each tale being altered and manipulated for personal gain."

While I was trying to focus my search on more impartial media, I wanted to get a less sterile and more vibrant feel for the information. I tried to concentrate on the facts that appeared to be verified by both perspectives, but that was very difficult. What instantly struck a chord with me was the revelation that our modern day Bible was a series of translations of translations, interpreted by the religious faithful who often received their information many times removed from someone who had spoken with, or was an eyewitness to divine encounters. I was also surprised to learn Jesus never penned any of the works himself, and his words and actions were always interpreted by one of his faithful followers. There were no signed copies of the original texts. I'm ashamed to say that I actually thought there was an original copy sitting in a museum somewhere overseas, and that it had been successfully translated into different languages over the ages. This, of course, was not the case.

I began to wonder how anyone could make any claims about the validity of the Bible if nothing could be substantiated. Without verifiable signed copies, how would you know the origins of any of the great works canonized for the Holy Book? Even then, how could you confidently claim it was the word of God? Based on today's conflicting ideas among people of the same faith, how could anyone claim that alleged feelings were sufficient evidence to substantiate that these writings from antiquity were divinely inspired or influenced? Especially after being orally passed from person to person, when the suspected author never had any first hand experiences with the miracles or events they were writing about? In a court of law, if I mentioned that I was sure someone had committed a crime because I heard it from someone else, who heard it from a guy who saw him do it, I would be laughed out of the courtroom. Especially when I couldn't produce these intermediary witnesses!

In the case of the Bible, we must add many centuries, dozens of additional people orally passing along and interpreting stories, and countless numbers of translations. We have all been the victim of misinterpreted circumstances or misinformation being passed from person to person, with many people embellishing, forgetting or outright lying about portions of the original message. Even if it were claimed that the eyewitnesses, Jesus or God himself had written the Bible, it wouldn't mean that it was true without supporting evidence.

The Bible does not discuss its own origins in any great detail. Moses is credited for the first five books, from Genesis through Deuteronomy, but he supposedly wrote about events that took place many years—or millennia—before he put pen to paper. With all his information attained through oral storytelling, songs and tales, why should we believe that it's accurate? We are left to assume his recounting of how the heavens and earth were created was simply given to him by God.

Obviously, there is no way to verify these claims. However, we all know Moses could not have witnessed the creation of the Universe, beginnings of life on this planet, the garden of Eden, etc. One of the most interesting claims I found suggested there were different authors for these first five books. With God often referred to by different names, and portions of text with separate writing styles. This appeared to be how many of the greatest works in the Bible were created. Multiply removed accounts of alleged eyewitnesses, which were passed on from generation to generation, not necessarily written by the authors the chapters were accredited to. Unfortunately, like many claims from history, our ability to investigate and authenticate information was very limited.

While reading through some of the biblical stories, I was surprised to find little mention from the authors about this coveted writing experience. I had assumed or hoped that every author chosen to write a portion of the holiest text in creation, while enjoying a very personal and intimate union with God, would have written a few lines about this honored experience. Unfortunately, I was unable to find much mention of God inhabiting the saints for the creation of this divine literature.

"So what, Ron, that doesn't mean the accounts weren't true!" says the believer.

You're right…but it also doesn't mean they were true, and with each amazing claim, I could not find any verifiable evidence to support it.

Then there were the similarities between the holy biblical writings and earlier stories. In the story of Gilgamesh, man's origins revolve around a magical garden, where the deity later decides he wants to destroy the world with a great flood because his creation had turned wicked. A vessel was constructed to save the animals of the land. Sound familiar? This story is believed to predate the one involving Noah. So why wasn't this epic poem mentioned during church service? Likewise, Minos of Greece would receive holy texts from his father Zeus on mount Ida, in the same way Moses received the Ten Commandments from God…or Mohamed received the beginnings of the Koran in a cave from the angel Gabriel. The practice of a deity transmitting holy texts in caves or on mountaintops to a single anointed secluded prophet seemed to be a standard procedure throughout many religions.

Now for more questions: How would anyone be able to verify these claims? Why weren't obvious similarities with older works ever brought to light during new members classes? How could anyone be sure they were the words of a divine sentient entity, and not the selfish or arrogant agenda of an individual? I could remain secluded for years, allege to have been visited by a sacred sprit that narrated a binding holy doctrine atop Pikes Peak in Colorado, and proclaim it as the New Word of God. But it wouldn't mean it was true. Even the story of Moses appears to have been borrowed from the Ancient Egyptian story of Sargon of Akkod, who was also set adrift in a basket to escape infanticide. Someone found him with ties to royalty, who raised the child as their own and he later became a great leader. Most surprising to me was the realization that several of antiquity's great leaders, prophets, and gods, all alleged origins from virgin births. Unfortunately, they are no more verifiable than the claim of the Virgin Mary giving birth to Jesus. I was also surprised to realize that if you really dig down into ancient history, you will find that early Christianity co-opted and augmented many practices and holidays from pagan religions, cults and groups. The parallels to other gods and other religions were amazing, with much of Christianity having close ties to the earlier Egyptian beliefs and practices. Even the story of Jesus seemed to have several strong parallels with the Egyptian man-god, Horus.

While reading rebuttals about these historic similarities, it seemed many religious leaders effortlessly claimed they were simple coincidences. But I couldn't understand how they could make such a claim with any confidence, when it seemed very apparent that these writers were simply altering stories from an earlier era. I assure you these authors would have spent a great deal of time fighting copyright infringement charges if they were around today! I would like to know what method was employed by the modern day theist to claim that the amazing, very similar stories from other texts were completely fraudulent, but the amazing stories from their holy works were undeniably true and unique?

Despite the apparent retelling of older stories, I pushed forward, investigating how the Bible was constructed. Many years after the death of Jesus, the framework and writings of the New Testament began. Over the next few centuries, several works were composed by various people, all hoping to be regarded as the binding holy texts. The most popular of these didn't take hold until about 144 A.D. when a man named Marcion came onto the scene. He was often in direct opposition with the church on many biblical points. He believed the God of the Old Testament was evil, and Jesus had come to save us from this malevolent dictator. It was very interesting to me that even a believer thought the entity portrayed in the Old Testament seemed a bit cruel. He also believed certain gospels to be the true word of Jesus and accurately documented his deeds and life.

With his own sense of theology, Marcion began to construct the first canon or collection of holy works into one divine doctrine. This quickly gained in popularity and challenged some of the long-standing teachings of the church. Church leaders became uncomfortable with the idea that the masses might follow his work as the word of God. So their solution was to construct their own canon. It took more than a thousand years, with each literary work systematically scrutinized and voted on for entry into the final manuscript.

This was the most surprising portion of my research. I always wanted to believe that each holy work would have some miraculous origin, with God seeking out an anointed individual from every walk of life to contribute to this holy collection of literature. But I was wrong yet again. You had to be religiously privileged, wealthy or connected for your work to be considered. Inevitably, this led to books never making the cut. I had always wondered why many historians and theologians claimed that books were left out of the modern day Bible. If God had truly inhabited the authors for a divine purpose, why would he have allowed men to deny entry of these blessed writings into the Bible? The recorded gospels of Mary, Mary Magdalene, Thomas, Peter and Judas, and several others, have been omitted from the great work for various manmade reasons.

With the majority of the population believing in the word of God without question, church leaders knew that careful scrutiny of this word would guarantee continued obedience of the masses. The church routinely manipulated scriptures and doctrine to simply push what they believed to be heavenly virtues, or what they considered preferred behavior for their flock. For example, Pope Gregory I revised a list of eight evil thoughts written by a secluded monk named Evagrius Ponticus into what we now regard as the seven deadly sins: Wrath, Greed, Sloth, Pride, Lust, Envy, and Gluttony. Interestingly enough, these sins aren't grouped together anywhere in the Bible. Yet, they were fed to the masses as the guiding principles of a good and righteous life. This artificially created philosophy was widely accepted not because it was presented in a holy book or decreed by a deity, but because one of the highest-ranking religious officials in the land declared its importance.

There was always dissention among the believers, with each sect or denomination questioning the others' motives and anointed leaders. For that reason, a might-makes-right attitude was employed by the religious leaders with the most clout. They quickly labeled anyone who would oppose them and their control as heretics, and mandated that they be conquered (usually by torture, death or forcible eviction from their home and land). Church leaders were also very careful to not only exterminate the leaders and disciples of false beliefs, but also any unholy writings, merely to prevent anyone from following in their misguided footsteps.

After weeks of research, I stopped believing the text was the word of a divine being. While the explanation of different men writing from their own perspectives was credible, it didn't explain inaccurate or conflicting information. How many off-spring did someone have? Were they alive or dead? What city they were born in? This major information would support the idea that much was lost over the years of oral tradition. If God's hand was truly guiding the writing process, it would have been a simple task for him to attain perfect congruency between every book and passage. While I can find countless books and articles on President Barack Obama that argue either for or against his handling of the presidency, none argue about the number of children he has, how old they are, if he's married or single, or if he's the 42nd or 44th president. For me, this continuous, fundamental inaccuracy really fostered doubts about the validity of the Bible.

In the end, regardless if Jesus existed or not, without evidence, why should anyone believe the claims of His divinity. Oddly enough, the one thing Islam and Judaism share is the belief that Jesus was not the messiah claimed in the Christian Faith. So it's not just the non-believers that question the divinity of the Christian God in human form.

I believe the origin of every spiritual doctrine needs to be personally investigated by the believer. Although I imagine many will prefer their comfortable place of ignorance, fearing what they might find would ultimately be too uncomfortable to accept. After all, if they have nothing to fear, a better understanding of its origins should only strengthen their walk with God.

When I started my research, I thought I would simply be committing a set of straightforward facts to memory. Clearly, I was wrong. At the end of my investigation, I was shocked at the complexity of the Bible's lineage. No matter how scholarly the author or how detailed the theologian tried to be, it was again the lack of evidence that made this information so difficult to amass. Guesses, estimation, and reasonable deduction were the only methods to piece together this intricate history of hearsay, misinformation and unrecognizable truths. Faith was again employed as the foundational framework for belief in each included work. Was a forgery passed as fact? Was a presumed misguided soul actually anointed? Or was the incompleteness of the story larger than we thought? The number of people that took a stab at literary greatness was exceeded only by the number of religious viewpoints that existed throughout its inception, and the amount of dissension among the faithful. Each ancient scholar believed his predecessor was ill equipped to do justice to God's unmitigated word. Writings were interpreted stories passed through oral tradition, augmented by the religious and political leaders of each time period. Plagiarizing from earlier works, and the systematic destruction of contrary doctrines, appeared to be a standard practice. Ultimately, sentencing the real truths of this origin story to oblivion. The canonized writings we refer to as the Bible today are the end result of the inclusion of writings based on power, privilege, and prejudice. They are further distorted by the self-fulfilling analysis of biased believers, and the evolution of text through many translations and alterations. At the end of the day… the doctrine appeared to be no more viable or divine than the devout believers that penned the work.

After researching the Bible's origins, I was amazed at how differently I felt about people quoting scripture. I again found myself examining every biblical reference with a critical eye. Most of the time I kept those observations to myself, but on rare occasions, I voiced my opinion by simply pointing out a conflicting scripture or alternate interpretation. When I did, I was instantly met with a shocked face, followed by an angry stare. To them, scriptures were the unadulterated word of God and should never be questioned. But I couldn't understand how I was supposed to believe the Bible was the true word of God when it was clearly written and constructed by men, and not by anointed disciples channeling their deity.

Even more peculiar, when I mentioned the atrocities and inconsistencies in the Bible, I was effortlessly told, "Well, things have been lost through the many years of translation." As if they had an original signed copy in ancient Hebrew sitting on their living room table! How can you simply claim that the parts you don't like, or the ones you can't explain, are just mistranslations of the original text, when you don't have an original copy to make such a reference? How many people have claimed to be abducted by aliens? Those people are still alive and can be easily questioned. However, we don't simply take their claims as evidence for extraterrestrials. We require proof of their experiences. I'm not saying the abducted are lying; I'm just trying to explain that we need substantial evidence for these amazing claims.

Now imagine that this story of otherworldly kidnapping was written in a book, by an author who was told the account by another, who was told the story from a man who saw this person being seized by aliens. Does that make it more believable? After becoming a skeptic, I realized that most individuals simply assumed everything they were taught about the Bible was true, without ever researching it for themselves.

Many Christian leaders effortlessly claimed that the punishments or atrocities handed down by God in the Old Testament referred to a very different time. They added that the Old Testament was only appropriate for the period in which it was written. This was said so the believers could begin to reconcile the apparent bad behavior in the scriptures. Unfortunately, God and Jesus still had very questionable behavior in the New Testament. Not to mention, there is not a single scripture that states that the Old Testament should be ignored after a certain year, or its relevance had an expiration date.

What *does* the Bible say about the Word itself? In Matthew 5:18, it says, *"I tell you the truth, until heaven and earth disappear, not the smallest letter, not the least stroke of a pen, will by any means disappear from the Law until everything is accomplished."* Add to that Hebrews 13:8: *"Jesus Christ is the same yesterday, today, and forever."* Or the words in James 1:17: *"Every good gift, and every perfect gift is from above, and comes down from the Father of lights, with whom there is no variation or shadow of turning."*

Incidentally, the idea that the Old Testament was period specific is only popular when trying to discount the Bible's atrocities. It is not observed when retelling the stories of God's good deeds. You can't hold up the alleged miracle healings, resurrection, or the saving a chosen people as a testament to his greatness, while conveniently ignoring or outright rejecting the notion of his questionable behavior. God's endorsement of things like owning another human being as property, advocating the murder of innocent women and children, or facilitating the destruction of all mankind, forced me to question the very motives and behavior of the deity at the core of my chosen faith.

UNANSWERED PRAYERS

One of the things I was taught early on in my journey for answers was to stay prayerful. During my time of confusion, prayer was my constant companion. I made it a point to pray in tandem, often asking friends and church members to assist me in attaining my goal of understanding.

Matthew 18:19-20: *"Again I say unto you, that if two of you shall agree on earth as touching anything that they shall ask, it shall be done for them of my Father which is in heaven. For where two or three are gathered together in my name, there am I in the midst of them."*

John 14:13-14: *"And whatsoever ye shall ask in my name, that I will do, that the Father may be glorified in the Son, If ye shall ask anything in my name, I will do it."*

During the prayer process, I began to really lose hope. I was told that anything asked in God's name *shall be given unto me.* So I couldn't understand why I was being ignored. All I desired was an understanding of God, and why I should believe in him and his word. When I asked for help in understanding why my prayers were going unanswered, I often received conflicting scriptures and advice from my fellow church members. It seemed like everyone had an opinion. There were dozens, each with a different meaning or intent, systematically working as a stopgap measure for the next. If my prayers went unanswered, there was a scripture or opinion to cover every possible scenario. Either I wasn't sincere enough, didn't pray long enough, or prayed for the wrong reasons, people, or outcome. I missed the answers, misinterpreted the signs, my prayer was unsupported by another believer, or my execution of free-will negated the blessing.

I remember one conversation with a church member after being frustrated for some time:

Friend: You may have not prayed long enough, or sincerely enough.

Me: How long will I need to sincerely pray before I get clearer answers?

Friend: Only God can answer that question; it's different for each person.

Me: Is he going to talk to me? Because that's what I'm going to need so I can have the clarity I'm looking for.

Friend: See, you have closed yourself off to the Lord. He will answer your prayers in his own time and in his own way! God works in mysterious, subtle ways. It may be a perfectly timed word from a family member, or the invitation to a new place of worship, or a simple demonstration of His presence in your life.

Me: OK, I see, I'm simply supposed to wait until I interpret His subtle signs in the actions of others. He's all-powerful, but never chooses to directly communicate with me. If it takes weeks, months, years, or decades, just stay obediently prayerful and eventually from sheer fatigue and desire to move on, coupled with spiritual nudges from friends like you, I will artificially fabricate answers out of otherwise everyday impressions or events.

This was the core of my issue with this line of thinking. I was unwilling to produce internal answers and equate them as the will of God. I was also unwilling to accept the idea that if I didn't get the expected faith-affirming answers, that I must have done something wrong. I needed evidence! Every Wednesday at the end of Bible study, I heard plenty of conveniently manipulated stories from biased believers who failed to ask impartial follow-up questions. But I guess that was the point. Like them, I was subconsciously being taught to ignore logic and reason when it came to God, because they took the majesty and wonder away from every faith-sustaining event. I was even expected to accept every major achievement in my life as proof of God's divine will, whether or not he answered my initially posed foundational questions. That's when I realized that prayer's power is simply in allowing enough time for the filtered interpretation of the believers to draw connections to random events, or facilitate changes on their own and simply give the credit to God.

Like an amateur scientist, I decided to run an experiment. I wanted to know how many different ways I could interpret someone's everyday events as a fulfilled prayer? Since many of my friends were in continual prayer about their careers, with most wanting new employment or better pay, I wondered how many events associated with work or everyday life could be manipulated to make someone believe his or her prayers had been answered. I began by inconspicuously asking my friends if they had prayed about their circumstances, and if they would allow me to pray on their behalf. Since most were devout Christians, they jumped at the chance. We prayed that God would make some definitive positive changes in their careers.

After a few months, I was completely surprised by the results. Almost every circumstance was thrown in the pot as God's will, and it was up to the believer to interpret the signs. This was when

I also realized I was getting four interchangeable answers for almost every circumstance:

1) Any Favorable or Good Event:

"It happened by the grace and glory of God's will."

2) Any Unfavorable or Bad event:

"God's great plan and timing work in mysterious ways that are simply beyond our understanding" or

"God's trying to teach you something that will lead to a different path or decision" or

"The Devil did it!"

No matter the event, I was almost always confronted by these four responses to bring reason or purpose to every experience in my life. This was also true when it came to my friend's prayers concerning their careers. Any promotions, salary increases, or newly acquired gainful employment was considered a gift by the grace of God, reaffirming their strong belief in the power of faithful prayer. If they lost their jobs or were demoted, God was trying to teach them to rely on him, and he was clearing the way for a new and more lucrative opportunity. His ways are beyond our understanding, but be sure it's all for his glory. Or the Devil was trying to derail their life, and they needed to rebuke his evil to get back on track. If they remained stagnant during the last few months, God was teaching them patience, and was still working behind the scenes for their big move. God's will for their life couldn't be interpreted or always understood, or the Devil was blocking their blessings.

Obviously, you could make up dozens of different scenarios and subsequent answers. From my perspective, if there wasn't a clear pattern or mark of intelligence behind an event, why should I ever believe it was the result of divine intervention?

Deciding on Atheism

So after researching the Bible, and tackling unanswered prayers, my doubts began to bear a closer resemblance to non-belief. I no longer believed the Bible was the divine word of God. The heartfelt testimonies and excuses for unanswered prayers were just interpretations made by individuals that in my eyes, were blinded by faith. So I turned to my last vestige of hope before completely leaving the faith, determining if a God really existed.

Many might wonder why I didn't start here. Quite frankly, I was afraid, too. It was one thing to disagree with, or not adhere to a particular earthly religion. But questioning the very existence of God himself? That was another matter entirely. It wasn't until I reached this point in my new walk of non-belief that I became comfortable enough to tackle this unpopular question. So I returned to the bookstore, library and internet, the only sources of information that had continually given me straightforward answers. While I know that this information is subject to some interpretation, it certainly provided me more answers than the ambiguous responses of prayer or faith. I also remember asking myself, what did people do before the World Wide Web? How much religious literature existed in the local libraries or bookstores that wasn't presented from a biased perspective? I didn't give it much thought and started searching for definitive proof of God.

It didn't take me long to realize that there wasn't any definitive proof for God. All the information I reviewed from multiple sources could only provide vague circumstantial evidence. Circumstantial evidence is defined as: Evidence that requires an inference to connect it to a conclusion of fact. In contrast, direct evidence supports the truth of an assertion directly, without the need for any additional evidence or a supplementary inference. Unsurprisingly, this circumstantial evidence was completely sufficient for the believer and insufficient for the non-believer. If you ask someone for scientific proof for God, which would stand up to meticulous repeatable testing, you quickly get answers like, "God does not have to meet man's idea of proof," or "What would be the point of faith, if he were obvious to everyone?"

But of course, I was done with these types of faith-based answers. For me, faith was no longer a reason to ignore reason. Many of my Christian friends asked, "Why must you have concrete evidence?"

My reply, "How important do you think the decision is to accept Jesus Christ as my Lord and Savior?"

They quickly said, "It's the most important decision you will ever make in this life or the next."

To which I answered, "Exactly! That's why I'm requiring *at least* as much evidence for this question as I would for anything else in my life."

While searching for answers, I noticed that every argument claiming to have so-called proof for the existence of God required someone to make huge unsupported assumptions. Or at best, these arguments only vaguely pointed to a God that was not involved in our daily lives. I will run through those arguments for God in later chapters, but needless to say, after weeks of study and research, I realized I could not be sure a God exists!

At this point, I became agnostic. I still continued the search for answers, but I no longer felt comfortable calling myself a Christian.

Over the next several months, nothing really changed for me. I just couldn't accept my former label, since I no longer held those beliefs. I kept the same friends and continued to be involved in the same activities, and I also made a point to visit other churches and mildly research other religions. But it became all too apparent that they were also based on faith. I came to notice that everyone I met seemed to assume I was Christian. I was often asked, "So what church do you attend?" before being asked if I believed in God, shared their faith, or attended religious services at all. I had never really noticed this cultural assumption until I was a part of the minority viewpoint. Anytime I mentioned I was agnostic, it was oftentimes met with confused looks. Many really didn't know what the term meant, and most assumed it was merely another name for Atheism.

Ironically enough, while sitting on my living room couch watching the *Discovery Channel* (I know; I'm a nerd), I was captivated by a documentary about the mythical ancient Greek Gods. How strange. I thought, "Why are these Gods believed to be imaginary, but the Judeo-Christian God is considered so real?" I came to the conclusion that I didn't believe in the Greek gods, but had no more reason to believe in the Christian one I was agnostic about. It was simply societal pressure that made me unsure and uneasy about claiming that the Christian God was not real. But I never seemed to have any problems believing that Ganesh or Allah weren't real.

That's when it hit me: I didn't believe in God at all. That when I compared his existence to anything I considered to be real, he was never able to meet the burden of proof, and I would never be able to believe in any God in the absence of evidence. This is when I realized I was an Atheist.

To this day, I have yet to meet a truly agnostic person. Even if they are an agnostic theist, believing that a deity might exist but his attributes are unknowable, or an agnostic Atheist, believing that even the very existence of a being is unknowable, they must ultimately take a position against all gods everywhere. Unfortunately, the agnostics I met were like me, only believing the particular God of their culture was unknowable. They felt perfectly comfortable openly denying the existence of Gods from other cultures, time periods and countries, even when the God about which they were agnostic hadn't presented any more evidence for his or her existence than any other God from antiquity or foreign land. When I ask the agnostic if they believe in Zeus, I'm instantly told, "No," instead of, "It's unknowable!" They are only uncertain about the God who, if they denied, would subject them to criticism or ridicule.

When I further examined the definition of agnostic, that the belief in God is unknown or unknowable, I had to ask myself in the absence of evidence why would I label something as unknown, and not non-existent? Why would I not be able to make a definitive claim about something that hasn't presented any evidence, the same way I had done with some many things considered imaginary. Why wasn't I agnostic about mermaids, or considered the truth of their existence unknowable? The simple answer was fear! No one cared if I didn't believe in mermaids, but boy did they care if I didn't believe in God!

Let's try a quick exercise. Take out a piece of paper. At the top, write the name of your God on the left. On the right side, list 10 things that you strongly believe don't exist. This might include fairies, Zeus, Bigfoot, Santa Claus, and other modern-day Gods. Now draw a line under everything you have listed so far. Under the make-believe side, list all the reasons why you believe they don't exist. Now apply all those same reasons to your God!

I challenge you to find a particular condition that your God could pass, that the known fairytales on the other side of the sheet couldn't. Remember, you must be able to demonstrate and prove anything that you think your God has passed. If the only difference is the faith you have in your God, you just believe it in your heart, or lots of people share your belief. That's not evidence, and would work for most of the things on the other side of the list at one time or another. If your proof consists of personal experiences, such as, "He saved me from cancer," then you have to be able to demonstrate that your God was involved in the act. Otherwise, you could just as easily say any God or anything was responsible for your supposed miraculous recovery. If you have to make a huge assumption, draw an unfounded conclusion, or your proof would work for both sides of the list, and everything considered fanciful, its worthless.

I'm an Atheist because I can't find any verifiable evidence for God, and certainly, none unique to him. I'm an Atheist because when I list all the criteria for existence, and apply them to God, he fails to meet them! This is why I don't believe a God exists. Can I say that with 100% percent unquestionable, absolute certainty, that at some point somewhere, something that we might call God existed? Of course not! But I know that this speculative God is certainly not involved in our lives. I can say that by utilizing all the rules of certainty that I employ for everything else in my life. I'm sorry, but I just couldn't continue to believe in a deity out of societal or cultural peer pressure.

Religious Discourse

After my epiphany, I made every attempt to keep my opinions to myself. I tried to do everything in my power to avoid entering into this often-philosophical debate. I became a self-proclaimed expert at changing the subject or giving vague answers that allowed my inquisitive friends to jump to their own "he's still religious" conclusions. I did not avoid spiritual debate because of any personal insecurity about my new title of Atheist, or an inability to wage a formidable argument, But from a simple desire to not be verbally attacked by believers when I was unwilling to accept faith, the holy doctrine or personal experiences as undeniable evidence of their God.

When I first became an Atheist, someone was always trying to show me the error of my ways. I was routinely presented with a slue of informal arguments for the existence of God, or reasons I should renew my faith in Christianity. The responses I loathed the most were the ones based on fear. While I was never quoted Pascal's Wager by name, something similar seemed to be always employed. Pascal's Wager basically states that you should believe in God because in doing so you lose nothing, and if he is real you stand to gain everything, an eternal life in his perfect kingdom.

But by not believing in him, you still gain nothing if he's not real. But if he were real, you would lose everything, an eternal sentence of torture and damnation in Hell.

"You just need to believe in God, so you can go to heaven. When you're standing in front of those pearly white gates and he's forced to send you to hell, you will believe then!" said many a friend.

This approach really seemed to bother me, and was always presented at the end of a discussion when they couldn't offer any credible arguments for the existence of their God, proof of his intervening nature, or evidence supporting their doctrine. You say I should believe in God just in case he's real ... but which God would that be? There are hundreds of belief systems associated with hundreds of gods. Why do you believe yours is the one true religion? Isn't that a bit arrogant? Why do you assume to know what awaits us after death, if you have never died? If you had undeniable proof of your God and the afterlife, you wouldn't need to try and scare me into believing in Him. Wouldn't an all-knowing being be able to tell the difference between sincere faith, and someone who just believes out of fear? Unfortunately, that's all I think your trying to do, frighten me into believing in him for a perceived personal gain. If I were to choose a belief system to follow, for fear of going to hell, I would choose one with the most likely chance of success. Another flawed claim made by this argument suggests that by believing in God, nothing is lost. But I personally feel like I've lost friends, that I was told to remove from my life because they didn't share my faith, countless thousands of dollars given away in tiding, that I did so even during times of financial hardship because I believed that I would ultimately be blessed. What about people who have killed, or been killed for their beliefs all over the world, it just seems like there can be a lot to lose by believing in God? Not to mention, if He would

banish me to hell for not believing in him, after failing to present the evidence and answers that I desperately prayed for in my
initial walk, even when I remained a good person after leaving the
faith, how ethical could he be? The only way this argument would
be compelling is if I already believed in your God to begin with!
If I told you Zeus would strike you down for not worshiping him,
you would laugh in my face. Why? Because you don't believe he
exists. So any threat of punishment associated with him would
seem utterly ridiculous. This is why I don't fear this supposed trip
to hell for not believing in your God.

When my friends or their religious leaders were not playing
the fire and brimstone card, I often heard sermons that directly
pulled on the emotions of their congregations. These feel-good
arguments simply catered to our overwhelming sense of self-im-
portance. Religious leaders would often ask rhetorical questions
that in the context of church, seemed to make perfect sense—but
were no longer compelling to me.

For example, they might ask, "Isn't it better to be the product
of an all-powerful loving God, who made us in his glorious image
with a divine purpose? Placed on a world constructed by perfect
hands in a Universe designed specifically for mankind? Or would
you rather be an accident of nature? A mistake if you will?"

Yes, of course being the product of a divine being would be
great (especially a demonstrably benevolent being!) I would also
like to think my bloodline comes from royalty and assures me of
an enormous inheritance in my future. But that doesn't mean it's
true. What about the ever popular, "Isn't it great to know you have
a heavenly father who loves you, and is always working on your
side, manipulating life's events just so you can complete your
divine purpose?"

Life is not fair! So while these feel-good statements are
preferable, they offer nothing as to their validity. Just because

I want something to be true, doesn't mean it is. I freely admit the prospect of not knowing where we came from, or where we are going, can be unsettling at times, especially to an often intellectually impatient species, but nonetheless we are still forced to wait for our coming-of-age answers. Unfortunately, because of our existing societal norms, some of us make up self-satisfying answers that can be easily understood at our current level of development.

The arguments that almost shocked me, but seemed completely viable to the individual, were completely ignorant of the points they were trying to make, or the information they were trying to reference: "Dinosaur fossils were put here to test our faith;" "The world is 6,000 years old because the Bible says so." "The cosmos was designed for us, regardless if we couldn't survive for more than a few seconds anywhere in the current known Universe."

When these are the best responses someone can offer while trying to convince me Atheism is wrong, I begin to shut down. In my early experience, I found there was often nowhere to go from here. They have presented completely contrary arguments to everything we have come to know about the world around us, and failed to offer any supporting evidence as to why. Their willingness to vehemently defend their faith with such faulty unsupported reasoning demonstrates an extreme prejudice to the truth.

From my perspective, the responses that always seemed to be clearly biased were those that undoubtedly showed a strong double standard towards what information would be accepted, from whom, and regarding what topics:

"Without question, the eyewitness accounts and amazing stories are accurate in our book, but not in anyone else's!"

"God's will is beyond our understanding, but let me tell you why there was an earthquake, oil spill, or tsunami."

"My God is real because he's involved in my life, but your God can't be real. You just think he's involved in yours."

"Miracles are a part of my culture, but are just strange coincidences or circumstances in yours."

"I completely believe in modern dating techniques to determine the age of the manuscript that appears to support my claim, but I reject them when they are used to determine the age of the earth, or dinosaur fossils."

I would often sit back in awe at how easily these people and others cherry-picked information. It was not until much later that I realized how widespread this practice was in all religious cultures.

In order to make myself more comfortable discussing the subject, I watched televised debates between theist and Atheists in an attempt to understand how I could intelligently and concisely explain my viewpoint without coming off like a pompous ass. Nor did I want to be perceived as someone attempting to convert others to my way of thinking. But I must admit, I was rather confused by the whole process.

This was all new to me. I was learning a lot of information to which I had never been exposed. For instance, I always assumed that anyone who used the term "God" was always referring to the entity preached about on Sunday mornings when I was flipping through television channels trying to find something interesting to watch. Of course, I was wrong again, quickly realizing that God means so many things to so many different people.

Obviously the God I was already familiar with, and is the most popular and widely accepted, was the personally involved guiding God. He is traditionally believed to have created man and our Universe. He is believed to be very much involved in our daily affairs, guides all humanity, judges the wicked and rewards the righteous, authors holy books, and more.

The second deity I encountered was the God of metaphor. The dictionary defines metaphor as *an analogy between two objects or ideas; the analogy is conveyed by the use of a metaphorical word in place of some other word.* Creative writers and novelists know metaphors very well; they are creative building blocks that create connections and new meanings between disparate objects. You might remember reading Stephen Crane's *The Red Badge of Courage* in school; within this novel lies one of the most famous metaphors in American literature: "The sun was a red wafer in the sky."

I always assumed that when people used the term "God" in their writing (even in the context of a metaphor), it came from very strong religious convictions, and they were purposely inserting religious overtones or wording in their works to pay homage to their core beliefs. I quickly learned that this was not true. The God of metaphor is simply a comparison (sometimes made by scientists) to explain something through analogy, and does not necessarily denote strong religious belief. For instance, on many occasions it was wrongfully assumed that Albert Einstein believed in a personal God or was a Christian. This assumption was primarily based on his use of religious language in his scientific literature, when this was done to simply illustrate a complex scientific idea. This wordplay became something Mr. Einstein would later be forced to clarify:

> *"It was, of course, a lie what you read about my religious convictions, a lie which is being systematically repeated. I do not believe in a personal God and I have never denied this but have expressed it clearly. If something is in me which can be called religious then it is the unbounded admiration for the structure of the world so far as our science can reveal it."[1]*

But in all fairness, Mr. Einstein also said: "A legitimate conflict between science and religion cannot exist. Science without religion is lame, religion without science is blind."

Many reading this passage might equate his use of language to a strong religious conviction, rather than as a metaphor for the

---

[1] Albert Einstein, in a letter March 24, 1954; from ***Albert Einstein the Human Side***, Helen Dukas and Banesh Hoffman, eds., Princeton, New Jersey: Princeton University Press, 1981, p. 43.

particular traits that each discipline brings to the table to comple-
ment the other. Some scientists might even applaud the speculative or exploratory aspects of religion in an attempt to find answers
to the big questions and its conviction regarding those claims. But
they simply differ on the evidence used to sustain and spread those
beliefs. In the summer of 2012, scientists in Europe announced
they had detected Higgs boson, the subatomic particle that the
media first dubbed the "God Particle" in the mid-1990s. The mys-
teriously postulated element may resolve certain inconsistencies
in some of the current models in theoretical physics. However,
it is not believed to be the ethereal genome of a deity. It became
apparent to me that many scientists simply use the word God as
a tool of comparison to describe the size, complexity and power
of a particular idea. So the expression, "The pyramids were the
result of God-like precision" does not mean a God designed them.
It's just a testament to the exacting accuracy of their construction.

The third God on the list was the deistic God. Deists believe in
a supreme being, but simply as the great architect of the cosmos.
He designed and constructed the Universe, then completely wiped
his hands of us. Deists don't believe in a personal God who cares
if you recover from illness, conceive children, or pray to him for
redemption, etc. This God simply designed the complex ship of
the Universe and then set it adrift on the cosmic sea.

Finally, the fourth version presented to me is the pantheist
idea of God. Pantheists believe God is the Universe itself and, as
such, is everything around us. He can be love, energy, earth, etc.

By learning about the different concepts of God, I better
understood the varied dialogue on this subject, and the formal
arguments for his existence. While listening to Christian debat-
ers and news anchors interviewing Atheists, I quickly realized
that many of the rebuttals I was fielding in my everyday conversations were the same arguments that were being utilized

everywhere: "You just can't get me to believe something came from nothing" (First Cause); "How do you account for the complexity of life?" (Intelligent Design); or the ever popular "You can't explain how the Universe began, so God must have done it" (God-of-Gaps). I will discuss each of these arguments in more detail later. But from my perspective, the issues with these arguments seemed obvious, and never provided consistent proof.

Some theists freely acknowledge that there isn't scientific evidence for God, and that it was a matter of faith. They proceed to try and defend the legitimacy of that faith. Unfortunately for me, I was looking for scientific evidence for the existence of God. Why, you might ask, was I initially looking for scientific proof, and not historic, philosophical, or moral proof? Because the very nature of science has made it the most reliable method for learning about the world we have ever devised. Not to mention these debates of believers vs. non-believers are often centered on subjects like the Universe, time, space, matter or energy. They draw in fields of study like physics, chemistry, genetics or biology, with theists systematically challenging scientific claims about the origin of man, the natural laws of the cosmos, or the foundational beginnings of the Universe or our species. Science appears to be the appropriate discipline to answer these questions. Some might say to me, "You're ignoring how God makes someone feel, think, or act." I assure you, I'm not. But science has been one of the most consistent ways of determining the credibility of claims we have ever invented. So let's prove that the catalyst is real before discussing how it makes someone feel, think or act. Does a man run because a lion is actually chasing him, or because he believes one is? How we proceed depends solely on whether their behavior is being generated by fact or fantasy. Do we call a psychologist, or animal control? The proven authenticity of the fixation is what helps determine the rational from the irrational, the just from the unjustified.

While reading through or listening to many of the arguments for God, I was left wondering why so many people seemed to spend an inordinate amount of energy trying to prove a deistic God. They were not deists, but theists. They completely believed in a very specific God, openly denouncing all others. They believed their deity listened to, and answered prayers, and routinely intervened in earthly affairs both great and small, that He conveniently and surreptitiously suspends the fundamental laws of science to perform miracles. This God seemed to sometimes get ignored in many formal debates.

The most published, debated, interviewed, and quoted Atheists often freely admits that there is no way they could have ABSOLUTE certainty that a deistic being could not have existed, at some point in time, at some place in the cosmos, for the briefest of moments. But that's also not their greatest argument. Their gripe (and mine as well) is with religions, and the belief that a Biblical, Quranic, or Torahistic God exists, one that dictates a worldview or reality in which everyone is expected to follow. I really wanted to hear evidence explaining why the God of the speaker was believed to be the only true deity. Why they believed in modern day miracles. How they would be able to make the enormous leap from a God that just existed, to one who sits by the bedside of every prayerful child. Or how the theist debating his faith could claim all of the other holy books were inaccurate or false, and why everyone should observe their particular system of belief.

By regulating an enormous amount of the conversation to an uninvolved God, it seemed to swell the validity of these claims to the everyday theist. By simply trying to prove that a generic deity existed, it filled the relentless emotional desire for answers to humanity's most plaguing questions, and could unanimously be endorsed by everyone with theistic belief from around the world. This would unite them against the critical eye of non-belief, allowing the common believer, who rejects the divisive claims of earthly religions, to uniformly stand behind this inclusive claim of a deistic God. But in reality, the apparent "good fit" of a nonspecific God ignored the varied stories, interpretations and specific explanations of how many religions of the world believe mankind and our Universe began. By simply miring this generic, all-inclusive, deistic God in the unknown he could be uniformly followed, and more easily believed by the masses. But I always thought this debate was between Atheism and theism, not Atheism and deism. As Richard Dawkins said, "We are all Atheists about most of the gods humanity has ever believed in. Some of us just go one God further."

Truth is, the distaste some might feel for my Atheistic position, they also share in grand fashion with faiths that are different from their own. The deistic God is harder to disprove, because the claims made about him are broad and regulated to the still unidentified origins of the Universe or man. This God is assumed to exist in the midst of things for which we don't yet have complete answers. So the Atheist is simply left to prove and illustrate the inaccuracy of the reasoning involving those few claims. But the theistic God, or the involved God of a particular faith, is easier to dismiss, because the claims about him are far greater and varied. This requires the theist to defend, or have explanations for considerably more material and inquiries. The lack of answers to this God led me to Atheism. That's why I was really hoping to see the conversations on this subject remain exclusively focused on the God in which the vast majority of the world believes in.

When I initially watched debates online, I had questions for both sides and was looking for answers. Unfortunately, many of the debates seemed to be pointless in answering my questions. I never understood why, in these often-formal settings, each side was allowed to purposely ignore direct questions, especially since the goal of the discussion was to take two conflicting ideas and explore the validity of each position as they relate to each other and the worldview. I've also never understood why some mediators stood idly by as someone danced around a directly asked question with the skill of a seasoned politician. Ridiculous or outright inaccurate comments were rarely challenged. When they were, each side simply claimed the other was wrong, leaving the audience to internally settle the dispute for themselves. I was frustrated by rebuttals that consisted of several minutes of poetically beautiful speeches that never addressed the initially posed question. Many seemed to take subjective traits like sentience, imagination, artistic creativity, or things like our ability to reason and ask how we could explain these without God's involved hand. How do we quantify these with the mind? In short, how do we explain the fact that our species is self-aware, complex and capable of so much? For many theists, God lives here. However, I was so tired of people employing dressed-up arguments from lack of knowledge.

I would like to see a debate in which each side gives opening remarks and then sits down with a mediator and their opposition to discuss the issues in a less structured manner. Maybe they can be joined or judged by a panel of people unsure about their faith, people with genuine questions. I would also like to see such a debate mediated by someone who would probe each question to its logical conclusion, and who was not affiliated with the mainstream media. Each side would be given a set of questions offered by the opposition, and then required to provide evidence for any points they would like to make. Long unrelated rambling would be stopped in their tracks. I would also like to see large Internet-connected video screens, with which a team of fact checkers would instantly verify, corroborate or refute a debater's claims. Above all, I want the focus to remain on a theistic God.

Surprisingly, there was one thing I realized after watching formal debates and comparing them to my conversations with friends or strangers. I would much rather debate a well-known Christian apologist than someone on the street. Solely because the lines of communication are more likely to stay open, since the apologists seems to be far more reluctant to defend their beliefs with the three theistic F's: Faith, Feelings, and First-hand accounts. Why, because those ideas are not backed by verifiable evidence. However, the layperson is happy to say it's all a matter of faith, that they just feel him in their hearts, or that they know first-hand God has touched their lives in some fantastic way. I often found it difficult to get past these all-inclusive stopgap measures in which the individual says there is nothing that could be said to change their mind.

Another aspect of these discussions that concerned me was the complexity in which the subject matter was being delivered. While both sides seemed well read and eloquent, would the layperson be able to understand the dialogue? During my research, I read Richard Dawkins' *The God Delusion*. While I thought it was a fascinatingly scripted text that expertly outlined the fallacies of the modern apologetic stance, I was left pondering who the intended audience was for such a complex read. With some people claiming a link between intellect and Atheism, and the scientific community comprised of predominately non-believers, I couldn't help but think this literature might fall outside the intellectual range of the masses. Even if there was the mildest truth to a relation between IQ and a belief in a God, would a book like Dawkins' be the Atheistic equivalent of preaching to the choir?

I remember a lesson from one of my teachers at Clinton Elementary, Ms. Stephaneli, as I recall: "If, in the first few pages of reading a new book, you find two or three words or concepts you don't understand, put the book down and find another, because its too hard." I don't consider myself an intellectual, but I never considered myself unintelligent, either. However, while thoroughly enjoying Mr. Dawkins' book, I remember on occasion that I suspended my reading to research either vocabulary or a specific theory he did not thoroughly explain, just so I could understand the overall concepts of some discussions.

By comparison, I've consistently been asked to thoroughly explain concepts and ideas when explaining my Atheism. On a daily basis, does the layperson discuss theories or scientific terms like abiogenesis, panspermia, *a priori* and *a posteriori* philosophical arguments, detailed evolutionary theory, the cosmological model, theoretical physics, origins of consciousness, determinism, or naturalism? Would I offer Mr. Dawkins' book to someone undereducated, whose conversational language never utilizes words with more than a few syllables? Or, worse yet, believes the earth is 6,000 years old? What about someone who believes human males have one less rib than their female counterparts, believing this proves Eve was created from Adam? Or the person whose idea of logic is that the unexplained should be credited to God? If Dawkins' intent in *The God Delusion* was to stir the intellectual juices of the theistic masses, I was curious to see how successful it would be. This is not to imply that the effect of the book was not felt at the intellectual higher end of the spectrum, routinely debated among the brightest minds on both sides of this argument.

Maybe that's the point!

The masses of believers at the bottom end of the cerebral spectrum will consistently believe what they are taught or told. They will continue to fulfill their role as blindly guided sheep, quickly mirroring any changes in the theistic attitude towards non-belief at the higher levels.

ETERNAL QUESTIONS

God is in every sense of the word untouchable; He's conveniently invisible, intangible, and firmly entrenched in the supernatural so as not to be bound by our legislated laws, or societal norms. He's not guided by mankind's ideas of modern morality. He doesn't have to meet any human standard for sentience or conciseness. He's never obligated to make any additional on-demand demonstrations, declarations, or predictions. He's Omnipotent, but his modern day all-inclusive pattern-less miracles are indistinguishable from luck, coincidence, or human perseverance. He's Omniscient, but his biblical predictions must be accredited post occurrence, with no prophetic mention of things like DNA, our microscopic world, or distant solar systems, and no simple documentation of our extinct Jurassic ecosystem. He's Omnipresent, so with contributory neutrality he is witness to global starvation, human subjugation, and oppression. Solely the product of faith, He will be described in vague terms with his behavior falling well beyond human understanding and considered completely mysterious. But of course, he should never be defied, questioned, or ignored, and always feared, followed and revered!

While searching for answers, I was often so frustrated with the untouchable nature of God and religion. Why was it such a forbidden subject when it was believed to play such an enormous role in our daily lives? Questions consumed me. They still do. Even today, when someone asks which church I attend and eventually find out I don't believe in God, they are appalled by my position, but can't seem to answer my most basic questions about the faith. It was this inability of Christians to provide concrete answers that led me to search for my own.

And yet, still many of my questions remain unanswered, and comments ignored:

1) The Bible is generally considered the perfect word from an equally perfect being. How was the book formed? By whom? How long did it take? What books were left out, and why? These questions are carefully omitted from new members classes and the church body as a whole. However, many fundamentalists argue that they want the supposed gaps in Darwin's theory of evolution highlighted in science classes.

2) You say we have free will, so why do so many believe the Bible is the perfect word of God and not simply the personal opinions of opportunistic men seeking power? Why couldn't the authors demonstrate any additional prophetic knowledge about our future world? Wouldn't the contradictions throughout the work point to the hand of men, and not the perfect hand of the divine? If the alleged holy authors were completely inhabited by God, and free will was suspended during the writing process, why would an omniscient God author divine scriptures and literature that he knew would later be omitted from the final canon? Or leave his questionable behavior unexplained? I also wondered why the churches of that time period passionately disagreed on which texts should be included into the final work. Wouldn't they all get a clear message from God? If they did get such a message and chose

to ignore it, why couldn't these supposedly anointed authors make that same choice?

3) You believe that religious eyewitness accounts are valid, even in the absence of verifiable evidence. You claim the Bible is a collection of recounted events by eyewitnesses that passed their story to others that wrote it down. But you won't accept first-hand eyewitness accounts of people who saw a flying saucer, the Loch Ness monster or mermaids. Not to mention many other religious doctrines can make the same eyewitness claims, but its utter nonsense when made by an outsider. Why?

4) "Miracle" is the name believers give the event. "The supernatural" is the means by which they claim it occurred. But I'm confused; the word supernatural is thrown around as if that explains everything with exacting detail. This term seems to refer to events outside the natural world, involving occurrences that supersede or violate established scientific laws. I'm fine with that ...but where's the evidence? They say God is eternal and formed the Universe from nothing, but how do you know that? Simply reciting the phrase, "It was a supernatural event," after science offers its genuine answer of "we don't know yet" does not constitute evidence. Think about it: today's easily explainable events like earthquakes, disease, thunder and lightning were considered supernatural in antiquity. To me, supernatural events have always turned out to be undiscovered or unaccredited natural events, or never existed at all. Supernatural events, once fully understood, seem to always fall into two categories: mythology or science.

5) I'm told that God's presence and the disciple's faith were so strong after the resurrection that people were willing to die for their beliefs, ultimately proving their beliefs must have been true. Yet, martyrdom is carried out all the time in 21st century religious warfare—but we say deluded men, following a false and incoherent religion carried out these acts. What's the difference?

6) How did we all evolve from Adam and Eve into an extremely diverse population of seven billion people, with countless numbers of animal and plant life, in what believers perceive as few thousand years?

7) I don't understand how a 600-year-old guy named Noah was commissioned by God to construct the largest ship of the time. Then somehow gather two of every animal into this ark while working out the logistical impossibilities of food, water, living space, and instinctual behavior. All because our super benevolent GOD was pissed off at the world and decided it needed to be completely and utterly destroyed by water. Then through incest and overcoming a limited gene pool, Noah's family would repopulate the earth?

8) I'm told certain Biblical stories should not be taken literally and must be interpreted wisely, but when I ask how I can tell what's fact or fantasy, I am told, "Use the Holy Spirit." Doesn't this ignore the noticeable spiritual divisions in Christianity on a wide variety of subjects, all claiming to be communicating with God through this same Holy Spirit?

9) You tell me I need to believe Jesus was real, quickly offering Flavius Josephus as an example of an independent historian who confirms the life of Jesus. For a minute, let's ignore the extensive claims that it was a forged document. Why would he have only written a small passage about history's most influential figure of all time? Why would the most prolific person in history (Jesus) be omitted from the multitude of historical texts written by the majority of other major historians and cultures of the time period? They say, "History is written by the victors!" Through war and persecution, often destroying any trace of what they considered false doctrines, Christianity was victorious in spreading its dominance throughout the land. While this is a well-documented historical fact, I still can't find that same widespread historical notations for the divine life of their messiah!

10) I'm often told that if we don't believe the historic accounts of Jesus, then a large majority of ancient records solely based on eyewitness accounts would have to be dismissed or questioned. I agree! If they are not verifiable through other means, then their validity could certainly be questioned—and often are. If someone told me Julius Caesar never existed, it would not bother me in the least, since this piece of knowledge does not directly affect my life. No one walks door-to-door contesting the validity of arbitrary accounts from ancient history. Why are unverifiable accounts from religious history passed along as truths?

11) People work on the Sabbath, don't take virgin wives, and don't have slaves. They make graven images and use the Lord name in vain—all in direct opposition of their believed divine calling! Many theists are unwilling to discuss the topic of faith even when it's their expected mission to minister to non-believers like me. Still others follow a misguided or false leader prone to pedophilia. Many of these offenses are punishable by death in God's law. Many believers rely on man for your healing and the simple necessities of life instead of the faith within their hearts. Yet, I'm told, I'm the one that's going to hell, because I no longer claim this ideology. Isn't it more hypocritical to assert belief in these statutes, and not follow them, then to reject these notions and still behave morally?

12) If I simply ask a direct question like, "Why won't God heal amputees?" I get an answer like, "God doesn't answer to me," or "His will or behavior is not for me to judge; it is beyond my understanding." However, when these responses are offered from other religions in an attempt to answer your skeptical questions, they are considered evasive, manipulative and unreasonable. Why the double standard?

13) Believers tell me I'm closed minded. But when I say I will convert tomorrow, if you provide me consistent, predictable, testable evidence? Believers reject that sentiment. Then will quickly claim that without faith, I will never truly get it. If faith means ignoring reason, and obvious follow-up questions that require me to believe everything in the absence of proof, how would I know my beliefs were correct?

14) I'm told not to rely on my own understanding when it comes to God, with many theists telling me he's simply beyond my comprehension and that I won't be able to reconcile his actions through earthly reasoning or morality. But in the same breath, they will claim to interpret his will every Sunday, or as it pertains to real world events. So if not my own interpretation or understanding, whose should I be relying on or following?

15) "You don't get it. You couldn't have really been a Christian to begin with." So I'm told. Still others say I've shut myself off to God, "and if you would just open up to his grace and glory, that you would be able to experience the loving presence of the lord." These comments have always left me wondering, "What do they mean?" When I ask for clarity, I'm always told it's something that can't be explained; "you just have to feel it." This answer ignores the wide gap in Christian philosophy between its supporters, who all claim they feel it. Since he seems to bless everyone equally regardless of affiliation or religious tenure, why would there be a need? But if by "feel it," I am to simply assume any good events are examples of God's will in action in the absence of evidence, I'm no longer willing to do that. If you think I was never a Christian because I am now an Atheist, I respectfully don't agree.

16) When I was a Christian, I felt that everyday favorable circumstances were examples of God leading my path. If these are the types of experiences that I should be associating to God, I can't see why. If it's up to the individual's feelings on what

experiences are divine and which aren't, why is my interpretation that I haven't had these divine incidents so easily dismissed?

17) Since God is all-powerful and all knowing, he would surely know what it would take to convince me that he's real. What would be his reasons for not meeting my definition of proof, even when I have consistently outlined what I would require to believe in him? If he wants me to simply have faith in him, why did he give me the option to choose? Wouldn't he applaud my search for proof, since there are thousands of Gods all claiming superiority, and his first commandment is "Thou shall have no other Gods before me?" Why would he not provide evidence far superior to the many other supposed false deities? Especially when he seems consumed with the idea of being praised and worshipped?

I'm continually told, without faith it's impossible to please God. But I have come to realize that without faith it seems impossible to believe in God.

PART THREE:

Arguments for Christ and God

Nonexistence

Many of the arguments for God's existence were repetitive. Each time I opened a new book, I found myself ingesting the same basic material. I'd like to share some of the major formal arguments I personally encountered and why they were not convincing to me. Since these arguments have been proven fallacious on so many occasions, and in so many works, I will only discuss the examples of faulty reasoning or assumptions that stuck out to me. I encourage everyone to read through popular Atheistic literature for a far more detailed refutation of these arguments.

The first argument, and which seemed to be the most flawed from the beginning, was the notion that the non-existence of God cannot be proven. Anyone could make up something that could not be disproved. I could claim an Elf spoke to me, I saw a three-headed unicorn, or I had lunch with Elvis last week, and you would be hard-pressed to demonstrate that I was wrong. I could also be careful to explain each occurrence in such a way where none of its components would be subject to scrutiny, by simply claiming it was invisible, outside man's understanding, supernatural, beyond measure, or intangible. How many people claim to have seen and experience all kinds of phenomena that we would consider fanciful? But we have no problem writing them off as crazy, and admitting them to the nearest insane asylum. Why? Since many of their claims could never be *disproved*, why aren't they taken seriously? Can you prove the non-existence of an evil spirit forcing someone to commit murder? Could you prove the non-existence of fairies, Poseidon, or Zeus? Of course not! That's why Carl Sagan's words, "Extraordinary claims require extraordinary proof," have such relevance. If you're the one making an extraordinary claim, then the burden of proof is on you to prove your argument. Since Atheism is denial of the claim that a God exists, it would be a foolish claim indeed—except when pressed against the original claim of theism that a God does exist. So if I said I didn't believe in the deity "Devorppa," you would think I was crazy, because you have never heard of him, or anyone claiming his existence or omnipotence. The bigger the claim, the more evidence one needs to support it. Why is the burden of proof on the person making the claim? Because otherwise, we would be forced to give merit to any claim, ever made, by anyone!

By the way, "Devorppa" is just the "Approved" stamp sitting upside down on my desk. So don't bother looking it up.

PUTTY GOD!

While playing with a friend's five-year-old daughter, she held up a clump of putty and proudly proclaimed it to be a dinosaur. I looked back at this misshapen mass in her hand and playfully said, "That's not a dinosaur."

My comment apparently irritated her. "Yes it is!" she replied.

"That doesn't look like any Dinosaur I've ever seen," I teasingly said.

In sheer frustration, she turned back to her toy box and grabbed a plastic cast of a dinosaur. She hastily smashed the putty down into the mold, pushing and pulling the malleable substance into every crevice. After working for several seconds, she pried the putty from the cast and tossed the plastic mold aside that had so easily brought her mental image to life. She then gleefully showed me the finished product. "Does it look like a dinosaur now?"

I smiled and nodded in agreement as she kneeled down to play with her younger sister.

This interaction reminded me of my own frustrations when trying to explain to someone that they can't simply treat their God like a piece of putty that can be merely pushed into any gap in mankind's current knowledge. My little friend did a great job of making this indistinguishable material fit her preconceived notions. But it was not a real dinosaur. At the core, it was a piece of inert, featureless putty with no real substance, and without much effort anyone could have molded this material into anything they wanted it to be. It was her imagination that gave it real life.

To me, God is no different than that mass of putty and can be effortlessly molded into anything you want him to be! He can be the singular God of thousands of different religions and ideologies. He can be pulled apart into multiple entities in a polytheistic culture. He can be a God, Goddess or Demigod. He's the God of Islam, Christianity, or Judaism; or the God of the Mayans, Aztecs, Egyptians, or Mesopotamians. He's the God of many names: Vishnu, Ganesh, Allah, Yahweh; and of many domains: the seas, earth, afterlife, and the cosmos. He can be the God of metaphor, the great architectural God, or the personally involved guiding God. He is just as viable for Muslim Jihad and the Christian crusades, as he is for world peace and true Love. God can be anywhere, anything, or anyone you want him to be. He's a baby's smile, a beautiful sunset, a biologically engineered pathogen or a charismatic cult leader. He creates earthquakes and tsunamis, just as easily as clouds, rainbows, and waterfalls. He can be in the distant past drowning the world in water, the present as a hotly debated subject, or the assumed future rapturing his chosen people while judging all mankind. He is the Alpha & Omega, the beginning and the end, and all the while and completely oblivious to you. It would have been your imagination that truly granted him power, eternal life, and sovereignty over all mankind.

In his book *The God Delusion*, Richard Dawkins coined the phrase, "The God of Gaps." I can certainly attest to hearing this as a principal argument from many theists when trying to defend the existence of God. When the conversation of God or religion came up, it normally went something like this:

Theist: So what church do you attend?

Me: Well, I don't actually go to church.

Theist: Why not? You do believe in God, right?

Me: Actually, no.

Theist: Whaaat! WHY NOT?

Me: I just don't see any evidence that a God exists.

Theist: So where did the trees, animals and man come from? Who created the Universe? Did it come from nothing? Was it a happy accident?

Me: Well, there are several prominent theories out there, but science is not completely sure. The Big Bang theory is probably the most popular regarding the origins of the Universe.

Theist: So what you're saying is that you just don't know, so why couldn't it have been God?

From this, the "God of gaps" is born. But along the way, obvious questions are ignored, the most obvious of which "Why is it not okay, to not know the answer, yet? But of course the questions don't stop there. What evidence do you have to support your claim? Why does it have to be a God at all? Why did the Universe need to be created and not formed through a natural process? Why would God and nothing else be the reason for this creation? Why would it be the Judeo-Christian God, rather than Allah, Ganesh, or any of the thousands of other deities? Why can't the creator be an alien life form from another Universe, billons of years more advanced than we are, or a green-eyed monster, all-powerful super computer, or the infamous flying spaghetti monster? The point is that there is no evidence to support the idea that it had to be a God, and certainly not your God.

This argument has always seemed so odd to me! The fact we don't have an answer for a particular phenomena does not mean that we can make an assumption or provide the generic response that "God must have done it" without any supporting evidence.

I have always likened this line of thinking to the same mindset that probably helped solidify the existence of some of the earliest deities: "Hey, what's this strange electrical discharge during storms?" "I don't know, must be a God throwing lightning bolts from the heavens." "I wonder what the big ball of light is in the sky?" "I don't know, it must be GOD. Let's worship it!"

One of the things that have always troubled me about inserting God into every scientific gap is the ridiculously unfair pressure placed on Atheists to provide readily available, highly detailed, verifiable answers to every possible inquiry. If I'm presented with a question in which the answer does not immediately come to mind, my adversary instantly invokes God to fill *my* personal gap in knowledge. This is one of the reasons why many Atheists I know are still educating themselves on the most popular arguments well after they have comfortably come to the conclusion that a God does not exist. They do so to remain knowledgeable and credible in the eyes of their religious critics. Someone might say, "But Ron, you're requiring verifiable answers from the religious masses. Why can't they make the same request of you?"

There's a difference. I don't expect the theist to walk around with the entire wealth of religious knowledge committed to memory, however I often feel like that is the expectation placed on me. For example, if I'm asked the name of each intermediary species in the evolutionary track that gave rise to modern day homosapiens, and I'm unable to name and describe each transitional form in exacting detail, the question is deemed unanswerable, leaving the believer free to evoke God as the cause, regardless of the fact that if given access to the internet and a library for a few days, I could begin to give them a credible answer. The reason I left religion was because my questions could never be answered, regardless of how much time or resources were employed. I was always required to make an illogical assumption or take something on faith.

The only thing I'm requesting of the religious masses is to provide basic answers to the most fundamental questions about their given religions, which they are passing off as fact. Especially when they were actively condemning others for not believing as they do, and trying to legislate their way of life. I was always looking for someone to answer the following questions without employing the Bible or the three theistic F's. You can't use the Bible as a primary defense, because the remarkable claims like the parting of the Red Sea, Noah's Ark, or even its supposed divine origin, cannot be verified. An occurrence written in a book is not evidence —especially when it is often written years or decades after the fact. Remember, if you run with that level of proof, it would also mean that the Qur'an's assessment that Jesus was not divine, and all who believed he was would go to hell, would be just as valid.

Nor was I going to accept the all-inclusive answer of faith. Which faith should I consider following, faith of the people in power, the oldest faith? Would it also be fair for science to deploy "REASON" as an equivalent grand answer? I was also not going to acknowledge feelings as a valid response to any questions, especially since that claim quickly ignores that strong feelings have been felt by every culture about every God. Lastly, because of its biased, pattern-less, conflicting and unsubstantiated nature, I could not accept personal experience as an answer.

With that said, I would love to receive the answers for the following:

• What testable, predictable, and consistent evidence do you have for the existence of God, Heaven or Hell?

• How do we know Mary was a virgin when she gave birth to Jesus?

• How do we know Jesus was the messiah responsible for many of the alleged miracles in the Bible? How do we know he died for all our sins and rose again three days later?

These were fundamental questions to which I searched for answers from my first days in church.

Modern science is still in its infancy, and its practitioners have freely admitted this. However, they are not making up an untested answer and pushing those beliefs on others.

"Wait a minute, Ron, my child is forced to learn science everyday in school," say some.

You're right, but the science they are being taught is widely accepted in every culture, and is not based on blind faith. The scientific method is verifiable and consistent. The freezing point of water is the same in every country, not to mention any areas of contention are not leading to wars! Let's say history students are being taught Christopher Columbus was the first to discover America, and this is an area of dispute. While I certainly agree it's important to find the truth and relay the correct information. The answer to this question is not influencing people to kill each other, or telling others they should live their lives according to Mr. Columbus's diaries.

Since the beginning of time, primitive man has created explanations for strange phenomena they were unable to define or quantify. Man seems arrogant, and in general unwilling to wait for his intellectual or emotional development to catch up with the complexity of the question at hand. It has become far easier and acceptable to simply claim it was a supernatural event created by an all-powerful deity. This seemed especially prevalent and acceptable before the introduction of the modern sciences like astronomy, biology, chemistry and physics. Some of the toughest questions consuming our society may not be answered for quite some time: How was the Universe created? How did life begin on our planet? What happens when we die? All are great mysteries in need of answers.

However, I think the most irresponsible thing we can do is make up an irrational, unsupported, superstitious answer, and say "Case Closed." We have very good science to explain how the earth was created, as well as several cosmic phenomena. However, we are not completely sure on how the Universe came into existence, or how life got started on this planet. Again, that's the responsible answer. Honest science is humbly honest. Simply asserting, "God did it," is not evidence. Of course we should continue the pursuit for knowledge and answers by creating logical hypothesis and meticulous ways of testing them. But to claim an all-powerful being who wrote a book thousands of years ago with conflicting ideas, with help from numerous phantom authors espousing their own agendas, is the best source we have for all man's questions, leaves me a bit confused.

I sometimes laugh at the number of long-standing and well-tested scientific theories that are trivialized, simplified or outright dismissed by some theists. This is very often done without the religious skeptic possessing a basic understanding of the theory they've so easily rejected. I can't count the number of times I've heard someone say, "If we evolved from monkeys, why are they still here?" As if this was the knock-down argument that has completely stumped the scientific community. We did not come from modern-day monkeys; we share a distant ancestor with African apes and chimpanzees. Millions of years ago, the genetic lineage of that distant ancestry split, with one leading to the early hominids and the other to gorillas and chimps. But the real issue is, if someone had a genuine interest in finding out the answer, they could have done the same thing I did, and placed this question in a basic internet search engine; read a book on evolution; or consulted with someone more knowledgeable then they were. Within five minutes, they could have had answers from multiple sources! But the reality is they don't want to know. They don't want the truth if it didn't support their preconceived ideas.

That's why many Atheists are former Christians, or at the very least, know something about the Bible. It was often their pursuit of a deeper understanding of the Bible and attempting to verify the amazing claims within its pages that led them to a place of non-belief.

As soon as I mention I'm an Atheist, I'm asked, "You don't believe God created the earth and the Universe, so you don't believe in anything!" If by "anything," you are referring to a supernatural deity, then yes, you are correct. By definition, Atheists don't believe in the existence of a God. However, if you were suggesting I don't have strong convictions about my life, society, or self-defining principles, you would be very wrong. I believe in goodness, tolerance, integrity, happiness, mutual respect, rational thought, peace, etc. On a larger scale, I believe in the uniqueness of our species, the perseverance of the human experience, our ingenuity, determination, and diversity of our cultures. I continue to marvel at the inquisitive, explorative nature of mankind that continues to lead to advancements. I could go on, but you get the idea. In short, I believe in *us*, and our ability to accomplish without an outside agency. Barbara Walker once said: "Faith in God necessarily implies a lack of faith in humanity."[2]

Science hasn't answered all of man's questions, and I'm not suggesting that it ever will. I would also never assume I could explain every phenomenon, and I think that's a mistake a few Atheists are guilty of. While we are very quick to criticize theists for making outlandish, unsupported claims about unexplained phenomena, we are equally guilty of dismissing and assuming there's no merit in any of these experiences. Unexplained phenomena or events like the Lost City of Atlantis, alien abduction, or psychic abilities, may one day be rejected or accepted. Either

---

[2] Barbara G. Walker, in *Women Without Superstition* (ed. Annie Laurie Gaylor, Madison, WI: FFRF, 1997).

way, it's a mistake to assume or dismiss the validity of such subjects without further study. The real danger is when we fanatically worship these unsubstantiated claims, legislate those beliefs on others, ostracize the masses for having a different viewpoint, and allow it to divide our society. If religion were treated like Bigfoot, where claims were widely ignored until substantial, verifiable and consistent evidence were obtained, where non-belief in fairies, gremlins, or the abominable snowman was not seen as appalling, I think we would be okay.

Science and technology have been steadily challenging theology for thousands of years. With every advancement the church has been forced to reevaluate their position on several subjects in an effort to stay viable. Gone are the days where speaking out against the church would mean imprisonment, torture or even death. During that time, the general population had a simple choice: Accept holy doctrine and the will of the church, or die. Consequently, few people openly opposed their control, and needless to say belief in religion, and particularly the religion of whoever might be in power, grew exponentially. This reminds me of a quote the late author and social commentator Christopher Hitchens once said about the church (although I think he was quoting someone else). "They wouldn't have the power they have now, if they didn't have the power they had then."

Today, you might only see that kind of absolute control and fear in a dictatorship. Since America is a democracy, you're forced to convince the masses your view is correct and should be followed. Just a few years ago, the Vatican made a point to announce that belief in alien life would not contradict a devout Catholic's faith. Interestingly enough, during this same time, a specialized satellite was launched to search for earthlike planets. If the church stood fast on every assertion that science had proven false, they would have a hard time convincing people they were enlightened and had eternal answers. Even today, the devoutly religious are challenging any scientific theories with a gap in knowledge or areas of contention. Since there might be a transitional form lost from the fossil records, the whole idea of evolving from a chimpanzee's distant cousin is laughed at by some in the religious community. I will be the first to say that we need to continue to look for fossils. However, evolution is a scientific fact, and there is far more evidence for evolution than God creating mankind with magical powers, or his random decision to create new life. If you believe God created the Universe, or life on this planet, that's fine. But you have to support this argument in such a way that you can't simply omit the word God and replace it with Zeus or Ganesh, with the same validity and lack of supporting evidence.

If you continue to hide in the current scientific gaps in knowledge, what happens when an answer is found, and that gap is closed? What will believers do when they're unable to simply manipulate their malleable putty God into another gap in knowledge? I guess very soon, all of God's power will be regulated to the time before everything began, and after everything ends.

Intelligent Design

So the premise for this argument basically goes something like this: If someone came across a wristwatch on a beach, it's too complex to have simply happened by chance. Basically, intricate design implies the existence of an intelligent designer. Supporters maintain that our Universe, the earth, and human beings are too elaborate and complex to have formed by random chance. Some scientists support their belief in God by trying to point out that the complexities in our biological systems could not have come about by Darwinian evolution or by primordial luck.

When I was originally introduced to this argument, I thought it sounded promising. Was there some merit here? That optimism quickly faded after I began my investigation. I first assumed that proponents of Intelligent Design or (ID) had actually presented a valid theory with supporting evidence and experimentation that was being reviewed by the scientific community. That couldn't be further from the truth. Intelligent design is merely poorly cloaked creationism, formulated by the religious to push a specific agenda in an attempt to sidestep the political hurdle set up by the separation of church and state, which precludes teaching religion in public schools. So it was not only being touted as a religious affirmation of God's existence, but was supposed to be a scientific alternative or a secondary option to the Darwinian theory of evolution taught in high school classrooms.

This weakly constructed pseudo science makes a complete mockery of the scientific method, solely because it doesn't employ it at all, with its supporters wanting to bypass experimentation, study, testing, peer review, or scientific criticism, and teach ID in our high school science classes as an evolutionary alternative.

Intelligent Design is a faith-based claim that enjoys support by playing into a believer's preconceived religious notions, and the fact that most people are not versed on the complexities of evolutionary theory. Despite the best efforts of many throughout the years, science and religion are not compatible. So, for many, ID and the Darwinian theory of evolution are also not compatible. Each student or believer would be forced to choose between God or Darwin, their faith or evolution. Since ignoring the latter doesn't carry any of the socially isolating ramifications associated with ignoring your faith, it's not surprising that many choose conformity.

"If you're a good Christian, you believe God created man, that's why Darwin's theory is wrong, and if you believe otherwise, you're going to hell," say some pastors.

In this context, of course evolution is the enemy. By exploiting the layperson's lack of knowledge about the theory of evolution and general science, the religious can sound extremely convincing. Simply because the average person is oblivious to the intricacies and many up-and-coming sciences like, genetics, microbiology, neuroscience, molecular biology, and biochemistry, that all continue to support evolutionary theory; or how lucky we are to have found as many fossils of transitional forms, which freeze in time the intermediary steps in an organism's evolution. Interestingly enough, there is no dissension among the world's most reputable evolutionary scientists about how life evolved on this planet. That's always seemed rather strange to me. Complex math is left to mathematicians, history to historians, biology to biologists, but evolutionary science should be left to the common man with a religious agenda and no evolutionary expertise?

I have never understood why someone who believes they have come up with the most comprehensive foolproof evidence for God or ID, hasn't written a peer reviewed, published paper on their findings and stunned the scientific community with their insight! Why aren't they silencing their opposition with this newfound knowledge? As obvious as it may sound, just because you spoke with your neighbor or fellow church member, and they seemed awed by your brilliance doesn't mean you have invented a great argument. For those who believe they have the answers, why not debate someone considered an expert in whatever field you would be turning on its head. In an age where our school systems continually rank lower than ever among developed countries, do we really want to confuse our students about what constitutes real science and what doesn't?

I've heard many argue that Science doesn't have any answers because they can only come up with theories. Given the credentials and the vast education of some of the theists making this claim, I can only assume they are purposely being intellectually dishonest. In high school, I learned that the scientific method, which gave rise to these theories, is based on a comprehensive framework of hypothesis supported by meticulous observation, experimentation, and peer review, etc. They are not some fly-by-night guess made at 3 a.m. after stumbling home drunk or battling insomnia. If this information was a part of my high school curriculum, I must assume that most of the highly educated religious apologists are also aware of these facts, and are choosing to ignore its relevance to push a specific message.

The biased guess of Intelligent Design seems to abruptly stop after the statement "We are the product of an intelligent designer." It is not enough to merely point out that some aspects of life *seem* too complex to have happened by chance, while never offering concrete, testable evidence to explain why. Simply asserting that the proverbial "missing link" has never been found is not sufficient evidence to bolster your argument. ID simply chooses to hide in the cracks left in the evolutionary framework. If one transitional fossil is missing among the thousands already discovered, this is somehow where Intelligent Design lives and breeds.

Unfortunately, ID and its supporters fail to answer the plethora of follow up questions: What expertise or evidence do you have to support this claim? Has the evidence you're presenting met any criteria, free of assumptions, and been meticulously tested? How did this intelligent designer create life? Who was this designer to begin with? Did this designer also create diseases and viruses that continually ravage his other assumed creations? If life is too complex to not have been designed, who designed the surely more complex designer? This, of course, creates and infinite regress of designers, so who was the original or eternal designer?

To me, this was quickly sounding more like a plug for God, and not an alternative or supplementary theory; and by theory, I mean the laypersons definition of the word, a completely unsupported guess. When I listen to supporters of ID, they seem to be preoccupied with simply trying to prove the original Darwinian theory wrong. I don't understand how successfully or unsuccessfully disproving one position or theory lends any credence to another. Don't you have to provide evidence for the answer you think is correct; especially if you want it followed by the masses and taught to our children?

You might ask, "But Ron, how can you ignore the complexity of our DNA, this is undeniably the fingerprint of God?"

If this is God's work, why isn't it mentioned in his holy doctrine? Why doesn't a single first-century prophet know anything about this crowning achievement in biological engineering? Why would there be flaws or imperfection in our biology? Why would an omnipotent being, that can produce life from a handful of dirt or nothing, need to develop DNA to transmit the data of life? How does the story of the human genome fit with the origin story of Adam and Eve? How was God able to create enough genetic diversity from only two people in the Garden of Eden, and again from Noah's family after the great flood? I don't see why unsupported claims, made while purposely ignoring the resulting pertinent questions, should be taken seriously.

For argument's sake, let's say our systems are indeed too complex to have been formed arbitrarily. I still don't understand why the default position would be, "God must have done it." There are other ideas on the table that could serve as a viable answer. One proposal could be that we are the product of an ancient advanced alien race that created life on this planet using their own genetics as a template. In 2010, the geneticist Greg Venter and his team created the world's first synthetic cell. Imagine what we'll be capable of a thousand years from now! Many will laugh at this idea. But again, this would seem like a better guess than Adam's origin from a handful of dirt.

Maybe the theory of panspermia could be true, where life evolved somewhere else in the Universe and the remnants of that life were transported to earth on a celestial body, seeding our planet in its infancy. In fact let's get really inventive, maybe the meteor that smashed just off the Yucatan peninsula 65 million years ago, killing the dinosaurs, could have given rise to life in a distant solar system by the same means. The genetic material from the cretaceous period might have hitched a ride on the debris created by the impact, floating through space for centuries until it seeded an early ecosystem of an earth-like planet. We might one day stumble upon a celestial Jurassic Park, in which the reptilian genome rose to sentient beings. But that doesn't mean they were designed with intent, or they should worship earth! Come to think of it, I might have seen that same scenario in a science fiction film once.

I've sometimes been asked, "So you believe that Darwin was correct about how life began?" I'm never quite sure how to answer this question. Again, it leads me to believe they haven't bothered to investigate the science behind the theory before so vehemently opposing it. Darwin's theory of evolution does not refer to how the first self-replicating microscopic organism came into existence. It only refers to already living creatures (although very simple), and how those life forms changed over long periods of time into progressively more complex organisms through natural selection, environment, genetic mutation, etc. If you believe God was the great designer of life, I don't have a problem with that claim, as long as your theory can stand up to the same scrutiny 19th, 20th and now 21st century scientists have placed on the original one made by Darwin.

This reminds me of a famous court case that divided a small Pennsylvania town. Several community members didn't like the idea that their children were being taught that God hadn't created man, and basically wanted Intelligent Design (creationism) taught alongside Darwin's theory of evolution in the high school classrooms. After much protest, the local school board decided to read a prepared statement before the science teachers began their lectures on evolution. It basically asserted that Darwin's theory of evolution was just that, a theory, and that there were gaps in the evolutionary argument. It went on to offer intelligent design as an alternative theory gaining support in the scientific community, and that textbooks would be made available in the library if anyone wanted to know more. The school board was quickly sued by several of the local parents and science teachers. This landmark Supreme Court case gained international celebrity, with many wondering if a loss in this case would instantly change the face of evolutionary education across the country. Because of the separation of church and state, intelligent design was presented as a scientific theory, and not a religious affirmation of God's existence.

During the trial, Michael Behe, a key defendant of ID, used the phrase "Irreducibly Complex." He was referring to the complexity of certain biological systems that he believed could not function, and would be utterly useless without all of its parts; therefore, they must have been designed. He pointed to the bacterial flagella motor as a key example. It was described as a tiny outboard motor of the microscopic world, used by bacteria to navigate their environment by whipping around and propelling the organism forward. Unfortunately for him, the whole argument rested on the idea that this irreducibly complex, intelligently designed component would be useless if even one of its elements were removed. This was proven wrong when a prominent scientist explained that many of the supposedly irreducibly complex organisms in the flagella motor are found in the Three Secretory System or TTSS used by bacteria to pump toxins into their host organisms. Needless to say, after many weeks of testimony, the intelligent design argument was exposed and dismissed as a repackaging of religious creationism.

In a way, I was kind of curious to see what would have happened if ID had won the case and became a part of the high school curriculum. I wanted to see what would have happened when the students began questioning their teachers during lectures. I can imagine what that dialogue would have sounded like:

Student: Excuse me professor; you have explained the theory of intelligent design and Darwin's theory of evolution, but which one is accurate? Why do we believe some organisms evolved and others were created? How does this designer create life?

Professor: That's something you will have to decide for yourself, but maybe both perspectives have merit.

Student: If they both have merit, how do we know where one begins and one ends? If there is a designer, how was he created?

Professor: I'm not sure. I guess where there are gaps in the transitional forms, you could insert the designer, and we just don't know who would have designed the designer.

Student: Isn't designer just another name for a Supreme Being, or GOD? If not, why would the religious credit God for creating us and not this designer?

Professor: Those questions are probably best left for your spiritual leader or the church to answer.

Student: But this is science class, and surely you're not teaching religion in science class?

You get the idea. How would we reconcile this untested claim alongside scientific theories that have stood the test of time and been painstakingly researched?

Many Christians want their children to challenge the notion of evolution in their science classrooms, with some parents and church leaders even providing questions that they can pose to their teachers in the hope of stumping them. I guess in some way, this was supposed to provide validity for their supposition of intelligent design. But I wonder if the religious masses would allow that same level of inquisitive behavior if it were turned inward? Would they be okay with teachers encouraging their students to question all of their held beliefs in their lives and dismissing the ones that couldn't provide evidence? I think this is really the disappointing part of this topic. We have an entire generation of children not being taught the theory of evolution in some areas of the country, solely because some teachers are afraid to touch the subject, or simply don't believe in what they are teaching.

Science doesn't concern itself with emotions, personal bias or agendas. In fact, it works very hard to filter out human emotions that lead to inaccurate information. This was the real issue I had with supporters of intelligent design, their lack of impartial non-biased examination of the claims they were making, and the fact that they sometimes tried to pass it off as legitimate or genuine science, ignoring the religious connotations associated with the argument. Anytime I've heard this argument referenced, it was either coming from a devout believer trying to justify his faith, or a religious minded administrator trying to justify a change in evolutionary curriculum. However, no one seems to be able to justify why the lack of understanding, concerning how an organism acquired certain abilities or traits, allows them to assume an answer without testing it. Why is lack of knowledge a justification for fabricating unsupported answers? Ultimately, ID supporters are simply saying they don't accept the current model of how some organisms developed certain attributes through an evolutionary process based in natural selection. They quickly offer examples of organisms that they believe defy this premise and deliberately point towards a God, most particularly the specific God of their faith. But in another example of selective scrutiny, they only seem to site or examine the life forms that they feel support their claims of a benevolent creator. From my perspective, they effortlessly ignore the complexity of pandemic-causing, disease-bearing organisms that adapt and become immune to any antibiotic, supposedly created by this benevolent entity. They reject the notions of panspermia or alien interventions as plausible answers for apparent design. They also dismiss the notions of other Gods being involved in our creation without explanation. But the fundamental part of this argument rests on the premise, since science hasn't figured the evolutionary tract of a specific trait or organism; we get to make up an answer that doesn't need testing, and it must be right.

I will never understand why every incarnation of homo sapiens believe it has all knowledge and nothing to learn?

I imagine a valid argument against any scientific theory would, first and foremost, involve fully understanding the theory to begin with. That enables the person to form a counter argument, collect and present the evidence that would refute the initially proposed idea, and possibly but not necessarily present a new theory, all in a way that can be tested and observed in a consistent manner. Saying you don't agree with someone, and not providing any supporting reasons, only illustrates your prejudice and ignorance. This bothers me the most about religious discourse when science is involved. When someone makes outrageous claims about science, and doesn't have the faintest idea about what they are talking about, or even worse, when they fully understand the concepts and purposely distorts the scientific claims to make it sound inaccurate or foolish.

"So you believe we came from mud, or a rock?" or "You think we came from nothing?" or in this case "So I guess dumb luck made us the way we are?" ask some believers.

In another example of lack of knowledge, some of the I.D. supporters only focus on a small part of the theory of evolution. While chance did play a role in our development, it was not the leading role. Even with my limited experience, I've come to understand that evolutionary theory is a concoction of different biological functions working together over millions of years. Natural selection is the meat of a process continually flavored by ingredients like genetic drift or variation, mutation, migration, environment...and yes, chance or luck. If you believe there is merit in intelligent design, then present your hypothesis, painstakingly test it and retest it, submit it for peer review, and then have your work published. If it's a scientific claim, then your data needs to be presented to that community. If it's a religious one, then I guess pass it along to all the great religious leaders of the world for their input. Science is the same in every country. Biology, chemistry, and physics don't differ depending on culture or geographic location. That's the reason why it's so widely accepted.

From our vantage point, evolution seems like an awfully big process. However, natural selection breaks down the process of complexity into smaller pieces. When you consider the millions of years we have been evolving, it's not as surprising to think we have become such complex organisms. Some similarities could be seen in our ever-increasing technology. If you consider where we were thousands of years ago, technologically speaking, it would seem extremely primitive by today's standards. Would the explosion in advancements during the mid 20th century parallel the supposed unexplained macroevolution in this planet's biological lineage? Could this extreme progress have only come about by the help of an outside agency? Did extraterrestrials aid us in creating our computer age? If our great ancestors could see us today, would they have assumed a God must have changed our world, solely based on the complexities of our technology and the fact that they could not personally understand how we made such great strides? Or would they assume we must have been given the plans for all our greatest inventions? Do you think we would be able to convince them that the smaller inventions and breakthroughs in antiquity gave rise to larger more complex technology? In this same way, evolution is responsible for the mind-blowing intricacy seen in our ecosystem today.

OK, I'm going to start teaching children they came from an advanced alien life form that visited our planet millions of years ago, planting the seeds of human life in a primordial pool of biological material. Prove that I'm wrong! This theory would completely meet all the criteria of intelligent design.

First Cause –
Cosmological argument

This argument basically states that everything, including the Universe, must have a cause. However, this chain can't go on forever, so there must have been a first cause, and we call that first cause "God."

Without knowing what laws that governed the conditions before the Universe began, how can we draw any conclusions? If you're claiming universal or natural laws don't apply to the condition before the singularity (Big Bang), then what, if any laws did apply? Why do we believe the chain of causality for our Universe had its origin or first cause just before the formation of ours? Why does the first cause have to be a sentient being? If it is, why do we believe it has to be a God, or more importantly one God in particular? Why does the first cause have to be eternal? And of course what caused this illusive first cause?

The first cause argument stems from a failure to ask any follow-up questions. It comes from creating a theory in which you already have an idea of its intended goal, which is to support the existence of a deity. God is of course assumed to be that first mover, based on Genesis 1:1 "In the Beginning God created the heaven and the earth." This is all the proof required for many Christians. Unfortunately, it's one line in a book and offers no supporting evidence. What if it were discovered that there were dozens of Universes before the creation of our own? I'm assuming fundamentalist Christians would simply back their God up before these events, and again claim he was its first cause. The reality is that we can't simply make an unsupported assumption based on faith about the origins of the Universe and wipe our hands of the issue. We can't claim God is outside this line of reasoning and doesn't require a first mover or cause. But when this eternal condition or existence is applied to anything else, like the Universe itself or the speculated multiple Universes hypothesis, it's instantly rejected without a counter argument.

I once heard a theory that claimed our Universe could be in a continuous cycle, expanding into existence for a very long period of time and then collapsing onto itself, which in turn expanded again giving rise to another Universe, thereby possibly making it infinite. I've also often been told that all space and matter came into existence at the Big Bang, proving that these things were not infinite. It was always my understanding that the true beginnings of space and matter are unknown, solely because we can't detect or observe anything prior to the Big Bang. The minute someone claims that something outside of our Universe is responsible for its inception, and that the laws are different in this void or realm, aren't they going to have to explain how they came to this conclusion? This argument is simply a hypothesis in need of rigorous testing.

"But something can't come from nothing, so the Universe had to come from something," says the devout believer.

I agree. In every case we have examined, something came from something else. But saying we don't know how the Universe came to exist is not the same as saying it came from nothing, especially when we don't know what nothing would even be. How do you measure nothing? How do you determine that nothing gave rise to something? Assuming our Universe is not stuck in an infinite cycle, giving rise to itself in the same manner that an uncaused God did, this argument only proves that something started the Universe, some how, by some unknown means.

So this is meant to be the all-inclusive answer that requires no more investigation? There is also nothing to suggest that this cause still exists. If in our experience we have come to understand that everything that has ever lived has died, can we conclude that any sentient life form that gave rise to the Universe could also be dead? If not, then maybe relying on our limited observation might not be correct. Just because we haven't seen particular characteristics in action, doesn't mean they do or don't exist. This is why cosmologists have come to the conclusion that the Universe's origins are unknown. They are not willing to construct an argument that contradicts itself, creates more questions than answers, and was formulated without any supporting evidence, and most importantly they aren't afraid to say, "I Don't Know."

Our understanding of time and space is still in its infancy, with new ideas and findings occurring occasionally. However, science supports their theories with evidence, and most importantly, reevaluating, augmenting, and if necessary, dismissing a theory if it's proven to be wrong! Christianity chooses not to do this. When Christians have a difference of opinion about their philosophies, they simply create a new denomination! There are currently dozens of Christian denominations. Catholic, Protestant, Lutheran, Orthodox, Pentecostal, Methodist, Presbyterian, Episcopal, Evangelic, Baptist, Southern Baptist, Jehovah's Witness, Unitarian…the list goes on and on! They have conflicting ideas about key issues: Should women be allowed to preach or not?

Is communion for everyone or just the church members? What constitutes a miracle? Is evolution compatible with our beliefs or not? Are gays immoral, or not? What are the appropriate ceremonies to honor God? Is hell the place popularized in Dante's Inferno, or the absence of God's love? Is baptism legitimate when you receive it as an infant or child – or do you need to accept Christ as an adult, so you can make a conscious choice? Some think a sprinkle of water is sufficient, while others believe you must be submerged. Some believe in exorcism, faith healing, and speaking in tongues, while others think it's phony. Some believe confession for your sins is an essential part of the faith, while others don't. Some believe Sunday is the holiest day of the week, while others believe it is Saturday.

Needless to say, the list is extensive. So is the variety of bibles available: King James, New International Version, Lutheran, etc. Christianity itself can't seem to agree on what's right or wrong. If there really were a God communicating with man through the Holy Spirit, you would think he would be able to send a clear concise message to his followers about his expectations.

ONTOLOGICAL ARGUMENT

One of the most popular arguments carrying weight with many believers today, but leaves me a bit confused, is the ontological argument from St. Anselm's. While the premise seemed colorfully witty, it was not convincing to me at all.

"*[Even a] fool, when he hears of...a being than which nothing greater can be conceived...understands what he hears, and what he understands is in his understanding.... And assuredly that, than which nothing greater can be conceived, cannot exist in the understanding alone. For suppose it exists in the understanding alone: then it can be conceived to exist in reality; which is greater.... Therefore, if that, than which nothing greater can be conceived, exists in the understanding alone, the very being, than which nothing greater can be conceived, is one, than which a greater can be conceived. But obviously this is impossible. Hence, there is no doubt that there exists a being, than which nothing greater can be conceived, and it exists both in the understanding and in reality.*"

Get all that? A very quick more easily understood summary might be:

"God is the greatest most perfect being that can be conceived or imagined, since he would not deserve such a title as an idea alone. He must exist in realty. Otherwise we would be able to conceive of a greater being, i.e. a God that exists."

I have never understood why this argument is so compelling. He takes a subjective claim: God is perfect or the greatest being imaginable. Then he simply moves on with his argument without offering any evidence to back his assertion. He never defines what traits would be required to be considered perfect or the most great, and then never demonstrates that the God in this argument possesses these attributes!

Could I not take any descriptive adjective and create a similar scenario?

For example, mermaids are the most beautiful sea creatures imaginable, because it would be more beautiful to exist in reality than simply as an idea of the mind. Mermaids must exist. Bigfoot is the most frightening creature imaginable, because it would be more frightening if it existed in reality than as a concept of the mind. Consequently, Bigfoot must exist.

I'm sure you get the drift. I don't understand how we could grant any credence to a purely philosophical claim as unwavering proof of a God's existence without a shred of real world evidence to back it up. Would this being not be the pinnacle of all concepts, that is to say, wouldn't the most perfect being be the highest attainable level in every conceivable trait of sentient intelligent or existence? Wouldn't it be the ultimate litmus test for beauty, intelligence, love, power, mercy, creativity, morality, etc? Wouldn't the effortless demonstration of these traits be more perfect than the assumption of these truths based on faith?

I'm also not sure how you could determine if any being had reached the highest level attainable in any particular attribute. How would you measure if someone knows everything, or can do anything? Would we associate traits like vanity, vengeance, jealously, or facilitator of fear, to this perfect supreme being? Wouldn't the most perfect being imaginable create only perfection? What does it mean to be perfect? If we can simply equate perfection with the trait of existence, wouldn't this entity be more perfect if its existence were flawlessly demonstrable as to be unquestionable? Wouldn't conceptual existence be superseded by actual existence and be trumped by a demonstrably actual existence?

Maybe I can't comprehend the logic of this argument, but I just don't understand how you can draw unproven conclusions and pass them off as truths by creating your own logic for your argument.

OK, allow me to run this experiment: Where would I start if I wanted to conceive of the most perfect being possible? First and foremost, his or her existence would be easily demonstrable, backed by every piece of evidence available, rather than an oddly constructed philosophical argument filled with assumptions. How about a being so perfect that he requires nothing from his creation? I've never understood why a perfect being would need anything from us. My being would not need praise and worship to satisfy a supreme ego, trading our very existence for emotional or spiritual offerings. He would not require monetary support to facilitate the operation or functionality of churches built in his name. For that matter, he wouldn't have any need for temples or churches. His word would not need to be interpreted by the chosen few. It would be simple, profound and seamlessly perfect, bestowed like a heavenly instinct to all, never usurping free will. Most certainly, my conceptual God would never use fear as a catalyst for obedience, or bloodshed in his name as a conduit to spread his will. He wouldn't need a doctrine at all, but if he did, it would have been written solely by the deity itself, and free of contradictions. Every story would be factually accurate and beautifully supported by every piece of evidence available. His or her moral and ethical standard would be eons ahead of its time, never endorsing or ambiguous about reprehensible behaviors like slavery, but unequivocally standing in opposition to them. The guidelines for life and afterlife would be free of logistical loopholes; he would recognize the finality of this decision and demonstrably negate the possibility of other Gods. He would intervene in human affairs with such obvious intent as to preclude debate, allowing his omniscience to identify doubt and instantly satisfy it with exacting accuracy, perfectly customized to the individual skeptic. Utopia would not be the grand prize in a religious crapshoot, but a birthright passed down from his benevolent perfection. You get the idea.

So I guess we are still waiting for the being outlined in this argument to show up, because I can certainly conceive of a being more perfect then the one portrayed in this completely influenced, biased guess from ancient history.

Miracles:
Perceived Intervention

Too many miracles are the most convincing aspect of a theist's life. The personal experiences they have with God seem to be what exponentially amplify their belief. For me, it has also been the most widely offered evidence for God's existence, and one of the most difficult to dismiss. If someone claims that God spoke to him or her in private, there's no way this could be disproved.

Unfortunately, trying to explain to a devout theist that the perceived Godly intervention in their lives is simply the product of an overactive imagination is impossible. It's difficult to get them to understand that this artificially created mind-set was introduced at an early age and, through repetition and habit, is convincing them to associate certain experiences and impression as divine. This started on a small scale, with many young theists first identifying with the little things. When they woke up in the morning and before the sun rose, or they simply made it to work on time, it was GOD! By identifying with the little things, it reinforces a belief in God's ability to make changes on a much larger scale. Remember the four answers that can easily be used for anything good or bad that happens in your life to cement this idea? The most important thing to remember is if anything good happens, regardless of its size, timing or purpose, you simply declare, "It's by the grace and glory of God." If something bad happens, the answers become: "God's trying to teach you something that will lead to a different path or decision"; "God's great plan and timing work in mysterious ways that are simply beyond our understanding"; or "The Devil did it". I have heard these four phrases offered in the midst of every situation in which I found myself. Unfortunately, most people fail to realize that there is no discernable pattern, and the answers could be used interchangeably. For example, if your parents had a car accident, it's simply by the grace of God that your mother lived, and your father was taken. Why? Because God works in mysterious ways, and your father had fulfilled his purpose on earth and was called home. God is trying to teach you to be an advocate for seatbelt laws, or that you need to stand on your own two feet without him by your side. The Devil was trying to take them both, but God protected your mother because she had unfinished work on earth.

I'm sure you could think of a dozen more scenarios.

Since becoming an Atheist, I'm sometimes bothered by the credit that is often given to God, when clearly great effort was put forth for a desired outcome. How many times have you watched the news and heard that a young couple has been lost in the woods for several days, and that an extensive search effort has begun? Local law enforcement, hundreds of volunteers, bloodhounds and the latest in satellite imagery are employed to canvass the terrain and predict a likely course and potential campsite. Many in the search party have gone days without much sleep and very little food. Meanwhile, the lost couple has erected a makeshift hut to survive frigid temperatures, rationed the little food they brought, and conserved energy whenever possible. They have also cut down trees and greenery to make themselves more visible from the air, along with using pieces of their brightly colored clothing to aid in their location. If they are not found before they freeze to death, killed by wildlife or die from starvation, God must be working in ways beyond our understanding. He left signs for the hikers to escape their predicament, but they just went unseen, or the Devil had his way. However, if they are located alive and well, it's instantly seen as a miracle by the grace and glory of God!

This has always seemed so strange to me. Why was it considered a miracle? Dozens or hundreds of people were looking for them, and they wanted to be found. Why are we taking credit away from the helicopter pilots that searched until their fuel supply was almost empty, or the local townspeople that stayed home from work, walking miles each day searching unforgiving terrain? What about the thousands of dollars that were donated to keep the search effort going? And why did God allow them to get lost in the first place? This question is always ignored. God gets all the credit and none of the blame. Why doesn't anyone ever ask, "Why did God put me in this situation in the first place? If I have upset him in someway, why wouldn't he just tell me directly?" Especially when someone is already a believer and has given their life to Christ. Why are they left to interpret his will, especially when it's so often considered beyond our understanding?

The strength of a religion comes from its followers. Some might say the only difference between a cult and a religion are the number of followers, and how far their ideology differs from the considered norm. Christianity was considered a cult at one time, and yet many Christians consider Islam's ideas and beliefs ridiculous. Still, no one can disprove that the souls of the 19 Muslim terrorists who were killed in the 9/11 attacks did not find 72 virgins awaiting them when they arrived in paradise. Or that the souls of the Heavens Gate cult were not transported away by an alien spacecraft, as they believed. But that certainly does not mean it must be true. Many religious cults have a charismatic leader that augments the meaning behind scriptures, convincing otherwise good people to behave out of character. Mainly because these followers are unwilling to impartially question, scrutinize, and research claims for themselves.

Many theists truly believe that God is involved in their daily lives. Quite honestly, I held the same belief when I considered myself a Christian. It wasn't until many years later that I realized that every resolved issue was a direct result of hard work or random chance. When I became sick, I didn't sit at home and pray I would get better. I sought medical attention. When I needed a job, I pounded the pavement, sent out plenty of resumes, and was interviewed multiple times. When I was finally hired, I simply ignored my effort and hard work, and proclaimed God had touched my life. When my brother stopped working at the twin towers a year or two before the 9/11 attacks, that was a coincidence, not divine favor. Although he's my brother and I love him very much, I don't believe his life has some calling or more value than the children, fathers or mothers that died in the disaster. I also would like to add that he's also not a believer.

Every perceived God-like intervention was simply my biased interpretation of my circumstances. God is all-powerful and omnipotent in every way, and yet the proof of his influence can only be seen if common or even not so common events are manipulated in his favor. Just like the followers of many perceived prophetic entities, believers must go through key literature and find a connection to major events in history after the fact! We are forced to do the same thing for God when it comes to his intervention in our lives.

There is no one on earth who can say, with complete certainty, they have done all they need to do as a good and righteous believer, and are 100% sure God will have no reason to not answer their prayer positively. I dwelt on this idea constantly in my early skeptical days. Based on my passionate obedience to God and unwavering faith, are there any guarantees to be granted prayers in which the supernatural event could not be misconstrued as intervention by man or blind luck? Unfortunately, my answer was no! I then assumed that I was not worthy enough to have such a prayer granted. So I replaced myself with arguably the most worthy Christian figure alive, the Pope, and again wondered if there were any prayers that the Pope could be assured would be answered by God, and therefore predictable. After all, if his prayers could never be guaranteed, what hope would the rest of have? Unfortunately, the answer was still no. The Pope has never come on live TV and said, "Fear not my children, I have asked God to simply clean up the oil spill in the gulf so it won't threaten anymore people, businesses or marine life." There is a good reason he hasn't, because he knows he could never be guaranteed that his prayer would be answered positively. I assume every stance taken by the Catholic Church in Rome was made with God's blessings, so by having God's ear, why doesn't the Pope simply ask God to use his omnipotence to provide the evidence so many Atheists desire? This debate could have been put to rest centuries ago.

If you pray to win a game, and you lose, it's simply reasoned away: God was trying to teach you humility, or he just works in mysterious ways, or the Devil had a hand in it. People often point to miracles as signs of God's will. Unfortunately, many of the sited miracles are just rare events or limited to medical manifestations. When cancer goes into remission, it's credited to God, even when that's the natural behavior of the infecting organism. Every time someone was pulled from the rubble days after the devastating 2010 earthquake in Haiti, it was considered God's doing, even when thousands of people would have survived if stronger building codes had been observed. We saw this a week later, when

Chili was subject to a larger quake and had a much lower loss of life. Just because an event is rare does not mean its eventual manifestation is evidence for God. For example, let's say only a small percentage of people routinely survive a particular disease. Why is it immediately seen as an act of God when we finally find a survivor? This is done despite statistics that implied we were overdue for a survivor.

Unfortunately, no one is going to look up the numbers or probability. Believers will simply see the survivor in a vacuum, and say, "God did it!" Inevitably their story will be continually retold to reinforce the idea that God is great and merciful. But of course when the reverse happens, and a good devout Christian is infected with a horrible and rare disease, no one ever asks, "Why did God infect me? Why wasn't the Atheist infected?" But we can simply invoke our three examples. God works in mysterious ways and it's unfortunately beyond our understanding. Just take comfort in knowing it's all-apart of God's divine plan. God is trying to teach you to be strong, and he is simply going to heal you and get all the glory. Or, this is nothing but an attack from the Devil, I will call the church and have Pastor Murphy lay hands on you Sunday morning and drive that malevolent spirit from your body.

My favorite assumptions made by some theists claim to understand and explain God's reasoning regarding major world events. Televangelist Pat Robertson alleged that the Haiti earthquake was caused by the Haitians' unholy pact with the Devil, and God was punishing them. How could he know this? Why didn't other prominent holy leaders get the same message from God? In fairness, Mr. Robertson is not the first person that has tried to interpret God's will, which has always seemed strange to me. If God's will is beyond our understanding, how can we try to explain his actions?

How many times have you heard your fellow Christians say, "God wants you to stop something, move somewhere, or get involved in a particular ministry?" I've never understood why the most powerful being in the cosmos needed to communicate through fellow church members, nor how his guidelines for my life seem to be in complete agreement with the messenger's personal opinions. How many times did you strongly disagree with your parents about a major issue, and they came to you the next morning and said, "Last night, God visited us and explained your situation, that your new purpose or path is a part of his will for your life. While we didn't initially agree with this change, we are now willing to follow God's will for your life."

You have to admit that it's odd that God rarely disagrees with you, unless you are using that excuse to explain your own failure or unanswered prayer.

During the past several years, gay marriage has been the lightning rod of a hotly contested debate, with many Christians standing on either side of this argument. My problem is, if there is only one Holy Spirit in existence, through which God is communicating his will, why do we have so many conflicting messages? Theists will simply account this inconsistency to hypocritical preachers. It's amazing that anyone who disagrees with you, even within your own faith, is simply dismissed as "misguided". I've also wondered why believers don't turn themselves in when they break God's laws. Unless they are caught in the act or about to be exposed, you never hear of pastors or church leaders appearing before their congregation and explaining that God convinced them they needed to admit to molesting children, committing adultery, beating their wives, or misappropriation of church funds. Why not? With their infinitely superior God-given morality, they would have instantly known it was wrong. I would also like to know why God would allow men to commit such horrible acts and then lead a congregation in his name, claiming to be a messenger of his will? When I asked these questions, I was simply told to have faith.

As we've discussed, faith is the all-encompassing stopgap measure employed by many theists in response to the unanswerable. This is always touted as the reason for their belief in the fantastic claims contained in their holy doctrine. But's lets examine this a little more closely. How faithful are these believers? Why don't they rely on God for their daily needs, and stop operating as non-believers. They seek medical attention from doctors who prescribe medicines that might have been created by non-believing scientists. They desperately ask friends and family for assistance to resolve difficult issues, never asking themselves what they might have done wrong to fall out of favor with God. They are subject to just as many social issues, natural disasters, recession woes, and general hard times as any non-believer. I remember seeing a caption online that read, "Nothing says faithful like seeing the Pope being driven around in a bulletproof glass cube!" If God is real, why isn't he showing clear favor to his flock?

Most believers will proclaim an absolute belief in life after death, insisting that they know for certain their deceased loved ones have moved on to a virtual utopia, where pain and negative emotions don't exist, where you are quite literally bathed in God's love. Since this is such an amazing place, why do so many Christians share our secular feelings about death? Why aren't they pleased to be able to join their heavenly father, and content to put their lives in his hands, or the hands of their anointed pastors, instead of the medical community? Why isn't death seen as a happy, joyous time? Why would theists actively pray for someone's recovery from illness? In his word, it says only God has power over the saved. So it couldn't be a plot from the Devil. So it must be obvious, that there's a divine reason behind the sickness. But surprisingly, when someone is ill, I don't find Christians getting excited and praying for their death. Don't they have faith in their God? Why do they deal with a secular world at all if they truly believe God will provide all their needs through Christ Jesus?

If God does exist, and is omnipotent, what harm would come from simply asking a few follow-up questions to your perceived miracles? Why doesn't God ever restore the limbs of amputees? Why doesn't he reveal himself in a clearly God-like manner, putting to rest all doubt? Why does he bless everyone when he is often considered a jealous entity? These are just a few of the questions I was told to simply take on faith.

Unfortunately, I was always left wondering why I should take it on faith. What's my rationale for believing in an ideology in the absence of evidence, and the presence of contrary evidence? If you're going to claim that intricate design implies an intelligent designer, then the haphazard, completely random, hit or miss circumstances in your existence don't point towards a sentient omnipotent intelligence pulling the strings of life!

THE SEARCH FOR TRUTH

At the end of the day, many of the formal philosophical arguments for God seemed to be irrelevant and too confusing for the casual religious observer. In fact, many with whom I spoke believed they were inconclusive and doomed to failure by Godly design. Claiming that God was beyond scrutiny, and any attempt to prove his existence by trying to sidestep the heavenly mandated test of faith, would be unsuccessful. It has become apparent to me, through speaking with them, that many everyday theists see faith as not only an intricate part of their belief system, but an absolute rite of passage. Going on to say that if undeniable proof or scientific evidence existed, believing on faith would lose its importance and be nonsensical. They insist that the whole point is to surrender yourself to God by placing steadfast, unwavering trust in him in the absence of proof. By working without a net, or letting go and trusting in the force by turning your targeting computers off (*Star Wars* reference), you pass an essential spiritual exam and graduate to the next level of understanding. To believers, faith is God's ultimate litmus test. It's this goodwill offering of faith, and the believer's conviction supporting it, that allows one to fully explore the essence of what God is. Some felt by searching for evidence, you cheapen God's gift of earthly and eternal life. In short, they felt that God doesn't need to show his identification or flash a badge before being allowed into their hearts.

To the believer, the most viable argument for God's existence is centered on the feelings they have about their faith. Many of the believers I encountered viewed feelings as the lynchpin of faith! It alone provides the validation for faith. Feelings are to the believer what facts and figures are to the scientist. They are the justification, the emotional data that allows people to believe doctrinal or religious claims. I think this is why most believers ask me to open my heart to God, allowing him in so I may feel the experiment that legitimizes faith.

Of course, from my perspective, without ever finding concrete undeniable evidence for God, the holy doctrine or any of the original claims about any faith, how can one justify believing in any religion? What would be the reason for not believing in anything or everything without evidence, and then hold others accountable for not accepting this construct? To me, the idea of religious faith is a construct created by men, with the sole purpose of counteracting the reality that there was no proof for their invented deity and a belief system meant to control the masses. It's a carefully designed smoke screen and distraction, or as Karl Marx said, "Religion is the opium of the people" or "Religion is the opiate of the masses." By also portraying this all-powerful deity as vengeful, jealous, and full of wrath, dispensing deadly consequences for disobedience, and linking his power to the governing bodies, they could ensure that belief in his existence would be non-negotiable and utterly unquestioned. That's why faith is the cure-all remedy given to the perceived illness of Atheism.

In speaking with friends and family, I'm sometimes presented with the argument that the God question is simply and utterly outside the scope of mankind's ability to answer. That by relying on man's knowledge, abilities or even science, won't allow us to answer a question that is beyond its purview. More simply put, if it's not observable, testable, consistent or predictable than it renders science inoperable and man's understanding inadequate. So the obvious question, which I'm still struggling with, is: if it's completely undetectable by every known scientific methodology, and beyond the cognitive abilities of all mankind, what makes anyone believe that the phenomenon is real? Wouldn't this undetectable thing match all the criteria for non-existence? How would we measure non-existence? This is probably similar to the question of how do we measure nothing, which of course I wouldn't know, because we only make this assumption of existence without evidence for deities.

At any rate, whatever we use to validate an immeasurable, intangible phenomenon is the very thing that can be scrutinized by science, even if the tool used for that validation is feelings. Because, we can still scientifically examine the claims made by these feelings to help determine there validity. If evidence is never found, why should we treat this claim any differently than the child who says a monster lives in their closet, or people in the Middle-ages that believed in witchcraft?

But most importantly, if at the end-of-the-day your argument maintains that humanity is just not in a place to make any determinations about the God concept, why do we operate as though there is this completely explained phenomena, which has expectations on our lives as individuals, and as a species. Either it's determined to be true in some consistently, observable testable way, or it meets all the criteria of being currently non-existent, and can be ignored until more evidence is found. I'm also not sure how we can speculate about anything beyond the initial hypothesis that a phenomenon actually exists, and place it in cold storage until we determine a way to test it.

The reality is an Atheist is never going to accept any claims on feelings or faith alone, primarily because we don't consider either a valid means in getting to the truth of the matter. It was often the search for truth that led us to reject the notion of religious belief in the first place, where many of us were searching for a reason to legitimize faith. We can't understand why, in the midst of a plethora of religions all claiming belief in mutually exclusive deities through faith, it should be considered a viable method for discerning truth. Most theists we encounter avoid the questions altogether by simply claiming it's beyond the understanding of men, that reason or logic cannot answer the questions posed by the soul of a man. They say science is a cold, emotionless machine with no ability to temper itself or incorporate the feelings that are a part of the human experience, and that only by yielding yourself to God, because of your deep feelings for him, may you truly understand him and his will.

This is where my confusion begins, and more questions surface. Are feelings a legitimate way of validating faith? How does someone, who is concerned with truth, use faith as a viable method to reach it? How does humanity detect or know something is real if it's beyond the measure of all humankind? How do you know something is beyond the grasp of science, reason, or logic? Ultimately, can faith be right or wrong, true or false? There must be correct answers to the questions of whether God exists, or if he influenced the writing of the bible, or is governing all mankind. So my question becomes: what method would we use to know which beliefs are true? For me, faith has not merely been the belief in something in the absence of evidence, but the ignoring or arbitrary dismissal of contradictory evidence. Faith is believing because you simply want to believe or were taught to believe. Faith can never be reconciled with reason, because faith is believing without reason or demonstrable verifiable evidence. As soon as you discover a predictable, consistent, testable reason for believing in something, faith is replaced by reason.

I recently spoke with a friend desperately looking for answers as it pertained to this question of God. After witnessing God's absentee nature on so many occasions she no longer believed that he was involved in her daily life. However, she still believed in a soul, and a divine purpose for that soul dictated by a God. She went on to say she was looking for truth! She had heard so many things and opinions while growing up, but wanted to know the reality and truth of the meaning of God. From my perspective, I wasn't sure how she would ever be able reconcile the idea of God, her Soul, or truth in a faith based system.

Nevertheless, I wanted to help. When I suggested starting at the beginning and working forward, systematically finding evidence for the existence of each part of this quandary: she told me I was being too rigid, and that she didn't need to start at the beginning because she believed in the existence of a God and a soul, based on her feelings. She went on to say that she strongly felt the presence of both, but was trying to determine the true nature of each. I didn't want to argue against her strongly held beliefs, so I suggested that since these were emotions, maybe she could manipulate or create an idea of both that she was comfortable with. She rejected this as being patronizing and stated that she didn't want some made up beliefs, but the truth! When I asked what method would she use to determine truth, she said she would just feel it in her soul. But when I made the comment that strong emotions are shared by conflicting ideologies across the globe, how would feelings be a viable method of reaching the truth? She explained that it only had to be true to her. She was only interested in personal truths.

I was silently shocked, because again if you're interested in the actual truth, how would employing a methodology of "it feels good or right to me" be comfortably considered true, without any qualifiers? Especially when that same reasoning would work for, or validate, almost anything? At the end of the day, if she simply came to a conclusion based on feelings, it would essentially be identical to manipulating or creating a truth that was comfortable —which I suggested in the first place. But I guess the act of not consciously doing it, and only creating it subconsciously, gives the perception of being less contrived or artificial, and in turn more comfortable.

How can anyone claim they are in search of truths, and not made-up personal truths if they only employ a decision-making process that works for everything and is all-inclusive? Anyone could falsely justify just about anything by using the 3 theistic F's: Faith, feelings and firsthand accounts. For me, personal truths, which allow many to believe in religions and Gods, are simply coping mechanisms to reconcile emotions of fear and anxiety in dealing with current reality, or to avoid critically examining their longstanding beliefs. Because the prospect of being wrong or creating doubt might jeopardize the placebo affect that faith provides.

Believers cherry pick and accept the claims they like, solely because it makes them feel good. They are unwilling to examine the inconsistencies in their given faiths. It reminds me of the famous line by Col. Nathan Jessup (Jack Nicholson) in *A Few Good Men:* "You can't handle the truth!"

So what's wrong with that?

Here is where I'm torn. I agree that if your personally held beliefs make you feel good, and influence you to do good in our society, I don't have a problem with them. Unfortunately, when it comes to religious beliefs, they never seem to operate in a vacuum. They are often sustained through very strong emotions, and too often those emotions affect their beliefs, and in turn are systematically affecting their decisions, perceptions and behavior, all in a way that can negatively impact others. So my question is: how do we preserve religious belief, the sense of hope and comfort it may provide, and eliminate the divisive outwardly harmful affects?

Unfortunately, I have never been able to find an answer to this question.

During my search for the truth, I was always very interested in the Atheist who had been convinced to reconsider their position on faith, and converted to some form of theistic belief. I wanted to know how they adopted Atheism, and what experiences or information convinced them to again believe in the existence of a God. I was hoping that by reading stories about other non-believers who had come to a definitive answer on faith, or had supposedly found the same evidence that I was searching for, would allow me to gain some clarity about my own religious uncertainties.

Unfortunately, I saw several issues with each conversion story. In many cases, they were appeals from emotion, which is neither evidence nor a reliable basis for truth. Each author simply insisted they felt the presence of the Lord while in church or interacting with friends. Purposely ignoring the fact that these claims have been made by every faith about every God in every time period. Others seemed convinced by what they believed were supernatural experiences or visions, stating that they saw angels, heard God's voice, or interpreted certain events as only coming from him. Of course, all of the visions or experiences were only observable to the individual, could not be reproduced, studied or tested, leaving us to simply trust the interpretation made by the person making the claim. While again asking us to ignore the reality that everyone with theistic beliefs has made similar claims about their personal experiences with their own deities. Many of the conversion stories had a noticeable lack of detail in their explanations. I was always left with follow up questions that seemed obvious, which often led me to wonder if the author was purposely omitting details from the story to avoid scrutiny. Richard Dawkins' is often criticized for not presenting the theistic side of the argument in *The God Delusion*. So I was very interested in learning those key arguments. Unfortunately, almost all of the literature I looked through provided me with answers that were either all-inclusive, unknowingly allowing anything and everything from mythology, plagued with gaping holes in logic, or were far too vague to be useful, where unsupported assumptions were mandatory to draw any conclusions. Many attempted to utilize extreme, but faulty analysis, wanting skeptics to accept any trivial unknowns as a marker of divinity.

There is an old joke amongst philosophy students: When a student is asked how the philosophy class is going, he replies, "Not too good. The professor can't get past roll call because the students keep debating on whether they are present or not!" While this extreme analysis might be encouraged and warranted in philosophy class, it can be impractical in our everyday lives. Most of us employ reasonable observation, information gathered through our senses, and critical thinking to examine or learn about the world around us. The problem comes when we purposely ignore the obvious intent of the task at hand, and make what was originally a simple goal impossible, like taking roll call in a classroom. By adopting such a convoluted and unsupported examination of a particular subject, it might require us to either accept every possible notion ever created, or dismiss every possible answer ever formulated. So yes, I could make up an infinite number of reasons as to why I might be present or not, like in the philosophy class example, but would they have any merit in the absence of evidence?

Of course this human existence could be a great facade, and we could all be plugged into computers like the Matrix. Our Universe could be an ant farm experiment, sitting on the desk of an immensely huge alien life form. Ninety percent of us could be holograms, programmed to believe we are alive, like a holo-deck character from *Star Trek*. However, without any proof or guidelines on what we can accept as a valid claim, or a claim worth investigating, we would be left to consider or explore every idea ever created because all would have equal merit. So I don't see why arguments based on contrived criteria that have absolutely no supporting evidence should ever be accepted.

I see this same methodology when I discuss the attributes or behavior of God. If I ask the question, "Why does God allow such suffering and evil in the world?" I get an answer such as, "He must have a divine reason." It only appears pointless because we are not privy to his perfect reasoning. Instantly, we are not allowed to employ the same definition for pointless suffering that has served us throughout most of our lives, and are forced to say, "yes, there could be an infinite number of possibilities unknown to us that might justify why groups of people are allowed to suffer," even when there is no evidence to support this assumption. We don't employ this type of reasoning in any other area of our society, so I'm not sure why it's viable here. What about my earlier question: Why doesn't God restore the limbs of amputees? God can have a perfectly divine reason that supersedes our understanding of everything, and negates the possibility of it being reasoned by us. But again, if you would never accept these excuses about any other Gods, why should anyone accept them about yours? For instance, what Christians would believe that Allah allowed the 9/11 attack on New York to succeed because it was a part of a perfectly divine benevolent plan?

The lengths some people will go to in an attempt to refute or win an argument has sometimes shocked me. They fully believe their interpretation is flawless and offer the most ridiculous unsupported responses to avoid admitting they are wrong. We have all met people like this. Regardless of what evidence is placed in front of them, they provide the most outrageous possible answer, solely because their pride or programming won't allow them to consider any other viewpoint. There are some Neo-Nazis that believe the Jewish holocaust that took place in Germany during World War II never happened! They describe it as a conspiracy against Hitler. But they never want to talk to survivors, look at the video footage, pictures, artifacts, documentation, or provide a rebuttal. They simply explain away the overwhelming evidence as forgeries. I see this same behavior when confronted by believers who are appalled by my Atheism—yet are unable to answer my follow-up questions. They simply say they feel it, or believe it in their hearts. Never having concrete answers to many of the questions. An Atheist is someone who simply says, "No, I need to know that what I believe is actually true. So I need to have answers for these very important questions." Atheists are not willing to make up an answer when it pertains to belief in a deity.

In fairness, this extreme reasoning is more common than you might think. How many times have you told a loved one they need to quit smoking, and their response is, "We all have to die sometime. I could get hit by a bus tomorrow?"

True. You or I could be run over and killed by public transportation within the next 24 hours, but the probability of it happening is so remote that this is not a claim worth observing. If significantly more people were dying from out of control buses than smoking-related ailments, the argument might be more compelling. Even then, why would you increase your odds of dying at a younger age by continuing to smoke, especially when it's preventable? It's simply easier to make an outlandish claim than to admit your smoking addiction, because you either don't have the will power to stop or don't care to try. So when the best responses I receive are, "I just know that the Universe was created with light from other galaxies already on route to earth," "Dinosaur fossils were put here to test our faith," or the ever popular, "God just has a perfect unforeseen reason why he has not helped some, and harmed others," I realize they are just unsupported excuses offered by believers uncomfortable with facing the idea that their beliefs might at the least be indefensible, and at the most be untrue.

PART FOUR:

My Atheism

WHAT ARE THE MISCONCEPTIONS?

Oh My Gosh! Stop asking me if I'm going through a phase, or worse yet, telling me I am, and then ensuring me that it will pass: Stop asking if I understand what it means to be an Atheist! No...I didn't have a life of hardship leading me to assume God doesn't exist because he hasn't been gracious enough to fix my circumstances. No...I didn't have a life of privilege leading me to assume God doesn't exist because I've never had a need for him or his hope. No...I'm not mad at God, anymore than you are at the stork for not bringing your next child, and No... I didn't see Atheism as a free pass to sin, because it's all too obvious to everyone that you can still do that as a believer. I'm an Atheist because I haven't seen any evidence supporting the existence of a supernatural being or deity, and certainly not one involved in our daily lives! This is why I don't believe in GOD!

Stop offering personal experiences, so-called miracles and faith as proof of his existence, especially when it would be utterly dismissed when offered by an opposing religion. Stop offering me rice cakes when I've asked for steak. Stop providing me circumstantial biased evidence, when I've asked for consistent, testable, predictable proof. Stop pretending that intellect and reason are the enemies of faith, when in reality they are the internal auditors of truth, and the Atheist is merely the whistleblower. Stop attacking me when you're uncomfortable about your inability to answer my follow-up questions and are consciously trying to hide your own doubts. If you prefer not to discuss it, fine! But stop treating me like a second-class citizen who's beneath you, worthy of contempt and discrimination, and then expect me not to challenge the faith that fueled this behavior in the first place. Stop picking a fight blindfolded, and then changing your mind when you realize you're outgunned, when you were the one that fired the first shot... and please, please, please stop ignoring your hand in all this! If it weren't for your overly hostile, browbeating responses to every innocently posed question all those years ago, I might have never decided to find the truth on my own. I may have been content to stay factually ignorant about my beliefs out of a sheer desire to be associated with what some believe is a loving and compassionate faith. I would even argue that most of the non-believers would leave you alone if your faith was completely void of divisiveness, intolerance, supremacy and violence, and that you consistently and actively policed your own, where religious extremism and discrimination was considered inexcusable. It's no accident that the most docile nonviolent beliefs like Jainism (often offered by Sam Harris) are also the least protested. The French author Voltaire once said, "Those who can make you believe absurdities can get you to commit atrocities." I'm frustrated with religious ignorance leading to a false sense of righteous superiority, and often unavoidable prejudice.

An unknown percentage of Believers: *"I don't want to hear anything that stands in opposition of my faith, no matter how valid, verifiable, or pertinent. I know I'm right because I feel it,*

and my Bible and God tells me so. Because I'm right, the rest of
you must be wrong and just don't see it. I pity your ignorance
and misguided existence particularly when an eternally blessed
life under God's loving cover could be yours! Until you're right
with God, you're bound for hell and should be considered sinful,
tainted, and most importantly unequal. It's my calling to steer you
onto the right path, forcibly if needed, solely because it's for your
own good!"

When I first became an Atheist, I didn't really understand
how this single assertion was going to change my life. Initially,
I assumed I would be able to state my non-belief as plainly as
everyone states his or her faith and move on. Sure, I knew it was
an unpopular view point, and I would be forced to occasionally
deal with someone who was uncomfortable with my position. But
I guess I figured it would illicit the same sentiment that someone
might receive if they claimed to be Buddhist, Jewish, Hindu or
Muslim, that my non-belief would merely be perceived as a different perspective, that everyone would be entitled too. I never
thought it would be such a big deal!

Instead, it quickly became very apparent that Atheism has a
very special place of contempt in our society. Almost anyone who
found out I was an Atheist instantly thought of me differently, and
I always felt like I had to explain myself to gain their respect, open
mindedness, and sometimes civility. When I tried to explain why
and how I came to my place of non-belief, they were only willing
to entertain the conversation as long as their ability to provide answers held out. After that, they would simply claim it was a matter
of faith and state they didn't want to discuss it further. This is what
I found so infuriating. Why was it okay for them to openly show
me prejudice or criticize my position, but when asked to defend
this behavior, they thought it was perfectly fine to opt out of the

conversation? However, I often felt like their intolerance to me was simply a result of their poor understanding of Atheism.

Many of the misconceptions that I faced stemmed from poorly constructed and unsupported arguments that my antagonists heard while in church or among other believers, but nonetheless passed as truths. So their motives to discuss the subject were not in pursuit of a better understanding, but a desire to convert me, belittle my claim, or validate their own reasons for faith. When that proved to be unsuccessful, they were not interested in carrying the conversation any further. I couldn't get them to understand that there wasn't any evidence to back up their misconceptions about Atheism.

An Atheist is simply a person who does not believe in the existence of a God. That's it, nothing else! No other assumptions can be made. This is not to be confused with an Agnostic, who believes the existence of God is currently unknown or unknowable, or a Deist, who believes God was a great celestial architect for the Universe and then stepped out of the picture. With many religious fundamentalists operating under a literal interpretation of the Bible, coupled with a strong belief system and long religious history, I understand why it's such a hard concept to grasp. Not due to any issues with comprehending the terminology, but out of the sheer difficulty devout theists have in accepting the notion that someone doesn't believe in the existence of a God, and one who is very much involved in our daily lives. Because of this inability, misconceptions about Atheism and other systems of non-belief remain prevalent among theistic communities.

Some fundamentalists believe Atheists must worship the Devil. Again, I think this stems from the belief that there are only two choices, Heaven or Hell, God or the Devil. Obviously this is not correct, if we don't believe in the existence of a God, why would we believe in a fallen angel created by this alleged omnipotent, omniscient being who couldn't foresee or prevent a heavenly revolt and eventual banishment of one of his own? Who ultimately becomes God's greatest adversary, obsessed with destroying his greatest creation while ruling an eternal realm of fire and torment? Ah...no, we don't believe that either.

Ironically, the most common misconception I faced was the perception that I really wasn't an Atheist at all! That I was just acting out, or mad at God after running into a difficult patch in my walk with the Lord. In all honesty, when I considered myself a Christian, I would make statements of frustration about my faith, telling others that I was not going to continue to seek a stronger relationship with God. So I have personally facilitated some confusion regarding my stance on belief. I also freely admit that you can find believers making knee-jerk declarations that they have lost their faith in God, simply because they have hit a spiritual stumbling block. They often retract their pseudo statements of non-belief when their faith is renewed. But these people are not Atheists; and if asked, in most cases aren't comfortable associating themselves with the term. In my experience, their initial statements of discontent tend to be emotionally driven remarks, brought on by the inconsistencies that are a part of most faiths. But statements like, "I don't understand what he wants from me," or "God and I aren't on the best of terms right now", which the temporarily frustrated disciple can sometimes make, suggests aggravation, disappointment, or indifference with God as a being.

If someone has reached the point of calling him or herself an Atheist, they are not going to anthropomorphize God. They will not attach human emotions and personality to what they now believe is a mythological character. Atheists don't believe in the existence of the being itself. So we are not going to be angry at something we don't believe is real or exists! We don't debate with God, or come to Atheism because we can't understand him.

That would suggest he's real, and that is not our cup of tea. The frustration you see from Atheists is associated with the very real religious people they encounter. Please stop assuming that we must be mad at God because there is emotion behind our words, insinuating that we secretly believe in his existence but are simply to afraid to admit it. When you debate or discuss other beliefs, do you secretly believe in the fanciful claims made by their faith? So why must we believe in a God, because we are frustrated by the very real prejudice we receive from the people who believe in his existence? How insulted would you feel if someone mockingly said, "You don't really believe there's an omnipotent being out there whose son was born from a virgin, and died for your sins, rose from the dead, and preformed miracles?" That's the same frustration felt by non-believers when the insinuation is made that our position results from extreme immaturity or deep-seeded denial.

The misconception about Atheism that scared me the most was the idea that it represented a grand evil scheme formulated by the Devil to take over the world. Or that it was a repressive ideology looking to tear down the rights of the religious masses. Atheism is just a label, associated with anyone who rejects the single theistic claim that a God exists. It's just a statement, and yet I often see it portrayed as an ideology, or evil agenda. I never thought that not believing in something due to a lack of evidence was a way of life, which had to be defended. This was a primary argument I heard from people regarding my Atheistic claim.

"What evidence did you have that the philosophy of Atheism is true?" grumbled many. This was often seen as the foundation-destroying question to Atheists. If you tried to inflate Atheism into something larger than it was, a philosophy set of commands or principles, I guess this question might have some merit. But since Atheism is simply a statement of non-belief, I don't understand the power of this question. This inquiry seemed to fall in the same vain as the question, "Can you prove the non-existence of God?" Again, the entire position of Atheism could not exist without the initial theistic claim that a god does exist.

When I hear people describe God's existence, it's identical to non-existence, except for the claims made by its believers. In other words, when something doesn't exist and is intangible, invisible, and immeasurable, it cannot be tested or observed in any manner. Since God's attributes were identical to the qualities associated with non-existence, I would never be able to prove that he did not exist. However I can, and often do, illustrate why the claims made about his involvement in someone's life are inaccurate, biased, or simply imagined. Unfortunately, every claim that was supposed to demonstrate his existence could never stand up to any scrutiny and was taken on faith without any supporting reasons.

Even if God hypothetically existed in a deistic capacity, not involved in our lives at all, this still could not be proven unless he began to affect our existence in some way so we could then use this affect as a measure of his existence. If you're the one claiming God exists, then it's your job to prove your case. The ironic thing is, theists have told me, "You must have faith, because you will never find concrete, verifiable evidence for God, and that's the whole point of faith."

When the Atheist agrees with believer that undeniable proof of God does not exist, we are criticized, and then told to take it on faith. But why should I begin to have faith in something when its attributes suggest that it does not exist? And why should I **not** have faith in everything if its attributes suggest that it doesn't exist. In other words, why have faith at all, and why not have faith in all.

When I told my friends that I was writing about my journey to Atheism, they had mixed emotions. Some thought it was a great idea, while others were offended that I would boldly write my story for all to see. In their eyes, I was parading my Atheism to the world, when I should be ashamed of it. As if it were synonymous with writing the memoir of a serial killer boasting about the lives he had taken! One even believed that the freedom of speech should not be extended to what they perceived as "unholy, evil literature."

Odd thing: I have never read a book on Atheism that discusses an agenda to take over the world, or has anything to do with it. I would imagine the books written by Atheists would only be a single page in length if they didn't spend an inordinate amount of time trying to answer the plethora of follow-up questions from the theist's perspective. The majority of Atheistic literature answers the questions posed to the Atheist after the statement, "I don't believe in the existence of a God". When someone claims to be a Christian, it seems to be taken at face value. But if someone says they are an Atheist, many feelings, questions and perceptions come to mind. This is what Atheists, like myself, spend most of our time writing about: Defining religious belief, debating history, clearing up misconceptions, debunking the arguments for God, outlining the insufficient logic, poor evidence or biased interpretation of scriptures or events, etc. Not outlining a plan for world domination. If I wrote a book on all the reasons I didn't believe in unicorns, you would probably think I was crazy. Why? Because the vast majority of people share this belief, and don't think a species of miniature horse with a single spiral horn protruding from its forehead exists. Atheism owes all of its celebrity or infamy to the size, influence, and passion associated with theistic belief. It was the intolerance, divisiveness, and hypocritical nature of religion that ultimately provoked non-belief and systematically the literature. And it was the believer's responses to the single claim of Atheism that provided the content. It was my frustration with the hypocrisy among religious believers, and one young lady in particular, that led me to question my faith and prompted me to write. I wanted to tell my story in hopes of trying to simply gain some acceptance for my position.

One of the most difficult tasks in my walk of non-belief was discerning the intent behind every question posed to me. During my own journey to non-belief, I was often frustrated by the harshly dismissive and almost aggressive stance I received every time I tried to pose what I thought was a valid and innocent question. Unfortunately, it was often interpreted as an outright attack on the faith, even when I considered myself a member of that faith at the time. My questions were only brought up in an attempt to gain clarity, not as an open challenge to the foundation of the faith. Now I was on the other end of the debate. I was the one being asked the questions, and it was up to me to sort out the innocently posed questions, from the ones that were simply personal attacks about my non-belief or me. I didn't want to ignore someone who was genuinely interested in understanding my position, simply because of a few insincere inquiries.

I also struggled with not reacting to questions that, from my perspective, were obvious, but genuinely believed by some. For instance, after knowing I was an Atheist for several months, one of my friends in frustration asked why I worshiped the Devil? While I explained that this was not the case, I applauded her continued involvement in my life. Up until now, she truly believed that all Atheists worshiped Satan. It must have been truly difficult to continue our friendship after she realized I was an Atheist. This was my personal struggle, not becoming frustrated and angry with someone who was simply spouting rhetoric about Atheism that they had heard from others.

Some of my friends wanted to know why it was such a big deal. Why did I have to attend freethinking meetings? Why does it matter? Going on to say, I shouldn't concern myself with what

people might think of me. My response has always been the
same: if it simply remained a thought, I wouldn't care. However,
thoughts become feelings, which guide actions, and that's what
ultimately affects society and me. I guess it was hard for them to
see how their faith had affected the lives of so many others. I tried
to explain that if they voted someone into office, stood firmly for
or against a particular legislation, opposed the rights of a differing faith, sexual orientation, or culture, they might run into some
opposition. If you attempt to purposely derail a medical advancement, safe sex initiative, or high school science curriculum—more
specifically countering the advancements in stem cell research,
condom distribution in Africa, or evolutionary education—then
I cared. Or if you surreptitiously denied employment, housing,
property, loans, or services, ignorantly justifying your poor treatment or outright prejudice of someone based solely on an opposing view of your unproven faith, was undeniably the reason why
I cared what people thought about me. But I personally believe
only a small minority of the religious population perpetrates the
aforementioned intolerances.

Which brings me to my next pothole in this road to acceptance: Figuring out a way I could help change the perceptions
of non-belief while keeping the virtues of religious faith intact.
The moderate Christian sitting in the audience of a formal debate
might walk away feeling confused. Not understanding why their
faith can't simply be something they enjoy and practice without
interference from others or being challenged by Atheists. Unfortunately, they often ignore the people in their midst that are
willing to hamper the freedoms of others over this issue of faith.
I truly believe the vast majority of Christians in this country are
decent, honest, very kind people, unconcerned about defending
or explaining every specific claim regarding their religion. They
are simply interested in mirroring the message of kindness and

brotherhood conveyed by their religious leaders. I would bet that less then 10% of the religious masses in America would be considered the Bible thumpers or extremists! Most are happy to leave the task of judgment up to their god and simply treat everyone with respect and tolerance regardless of their faith.

My question is: How do I address the intolerance from the few, without the masses finding fault with me? How do I stand behind the rights of the religious majority, while actively criticizing the actions of the fundamentalist minority?

This is not to suggest that Atheism doesn't have their more extreme, or outspoken individuals, often cited when I'm involved in religious discourse. Unfortunately, the most demanding skeptic or outspoken opponent will only remember negative interactions with your group. So, the Atheist who sounded arrogantly condescending in telling someone his or her loved ones were not in heaven because it didn't exist, or the belief system that they have been observing for generations is ridiculous, tends to close people off. This overshadows the non-believer who has been nothing but kind to them. I don't ignore the reality that there are some crazy, dogmatic Atheists, but the Atheists I have met are simply tired of being judged by a single statement of non-belief and not by the sum of their behavior.

While misconceptions will continue to proliferate in our society until people are willing to independently research information for themselves, I still firmly believe courteous discourse is the only way we will overcome these barriers.

THE CHRISTIAN MAJORITY

"Hmmm…what declaration could I make that would ensure the most traumatic life possible? What would allow me to simultaneously alienate myself from my friends, family, and community? You know…something that would subject me to prejudice, intolerance and anger, and I don't mean a petty trivial type of anger? I'm looking for utter hatred and disgust. I want someone to find out about this assertion, and see their unmistakable revulsion and distaste for my outrageous position manifest itself in their facial expressions, words, and behavior. I want to find some way of symbolically spitting in the faces of coworkers and strangers alike, while at the same time generating superstition, misconceptions and distrust. I want to consistently walk into rooms where conversations suddenly stop with people dispersing while irritably staring in my direction. I want to put my career, relationships, and support system in jeopardy overnight. But most importantly, this statement must be synonymous with a questioned morality, belief in nothing, and devotion to the Devil!"

Contrary to popular belief, these were not the words I uttered before becoming an Atheist. While the circumstances cited above can be unfortunate and an undeserved byproduct of the decision, they were not my goal. Ralph W. Stockman once said, "The test of courage comes when we are in the minority. The test of tolerance comes when we are in the majority."

Atheists aren't thrill seekers or rebels. We didn't come to the place of non-belief lightly or on a whim. We just couldn't reconcile the claims and inconsistencies in our given faiths. We also couldn't justify believing in something when the evidence wasn't there to support it. You never know how the minority feels until you're a part of it. When I was religious, I thought nothing of being led in prayer before every event. As an Atheist, the assumption that everyone is a Christian became all too obvious. We live in a country where the outward assertion of religious tolerance is the continual headline fed to the masses, but unfortunately buried in fine print is the assumption that this freedom of belief only refers to Christianity. All over the country, protests are still held against planned Muslim mosques. Many will say, in light of the events on 9/11, U.S. citizens are just not comfortable having Muslim places of worship in their communities. While I understand the source of this sentiment, I don't think it's a good practice to create laws, or have constitutional rights, that can simply be ignored when they become uncomfortable. If these were Christian church's being built a few miles from an abortion clinic that suffered a terrorist attack from an extremist group, it would have never been challenged. Not every Muslim is trying to kill Americans, and claiming that every member of a particular faith is inclined to extremist behavior, is prejudicial on a grand scale. I'm just afraid that by denying anyone their civil and legal rights based on your personal feelings is not only wrong, but could also be something that might get out of hand. I just don't know if we want to start down that slippery slope.

If a community decided they didn't want Japanese Americans as neighbors because of the attacks on Pearl Harbor, or a neighborhood decided they wanted to ban a particular race, based on gang violence or hate crimes, would these biased sentiments be considered legitimate claims? Unfortunately (or fortunately depending on your perspective), more than 70% of Americans considers themselves Christian. These taxpayers have an amazing influence over our political system, and any elected official ignoring their requests could quickly be looking for new employment. "Freedom and justice for all" has always come with qualifiers. Not too long ago, this statement only referred to the privileged, white, Christian, wealthy, connected, elite male. But it's now the 21st century and we have come a long way since then...or have we?

Being an Atheist, I hold a very special place of contempt in this country. I believe a study once showed we are one of the most un-trusted groups in America! This is often offered by some believers as a reason to avoid us and our message. In an environment where the overwhelming majority of the population are Christian, is this figure really that surprising? If I polled the Afghan society, would I not find a similar trend towards Christianity or Judaism, or even the ideals of the United States as a whole? Being in the religious minority has certainly been an eye-opening experience for me. I took for granted how someone of a differing faith would feel in a society where the majority of its population was so firmly entrenched in the Christian faith.

For instance, an Atheist friend of mine went on a job interview. Everything was proceeding wonderfully. She had a great deal of experience and was making a genuine connection with her potential new boss. Unfortunately, or fortunately (depending on how you look at it), she became too comfortable, and the interviewer started talking about inviting her to church, and began explaining how much God has meant to her. She asked my friend, "So which church do you attend?"

While this question should have never been asked in a job interview, the sought after jovial banter associated with a great interview tends to foster a sense of familiarity and connection. That's
when the restrictive stale interview becomes more of a fireside
chat. This level of comfort can sometimes generate statements that
anyone involved in human resources would otherwise avoid, such
as: "There are some really hot guys in this office!" But they don't
know you're a lesbian. Or "We're going to watch political prima-
ries at Mr. Murphy's house tonight, I know Romney is going to
stomp Obama." But they don't know you're a Democrat, and an
Obama supporter. Or in this case, "I love the Lord, and would love
for you to come to church with me." But they don't know you're
an Atheist. Does the candidate simply state their opposing position, and quickly change the subject? I think not! While refusal to
hire someone based on sexual orientation, political affiliation, or
religious beliefs is illegal, we all know it happens. Suddenly after
your differing assertion, you abruptly don't seem to have enough
experience, credentials, or appropriate skill sets.

By the nature of our position, many choose to conform rather
than face discrimination. Living in the Bible belt has meant that I
am exposed to Christianity on a semi-regular basis, simply due to
the high concentration of believers. Even my Christian friends that
know I'm an Atheist often engage in conversations in which they
make religious assertions about their lives. "What do you think
God is telling me to do?" or "Was this a sign from God?" and then
they look to me for some measure of agreement. Is this a blatant
disregard for my feelings? Or is it just a social norm in this southern environment and difficult to switch conversational gears with
the only Atheist they know? When we attend business dinners,
involve ourselves with sports teams, or participate in religious

minded communities, do we simply bow our heads and join in the customary prayers? Or do we opt out of the ritual, and brace for the follow-up questions and possible ridicule?

In our country, there is supposed to be a separation of church and state. However, we find Christian symbolism in many public schools, government facilities and courthouses throughout the country. Could this be misinterpreted as a message to people of other religions that they're not going to get the same level of treatment in these public facilities or a fair trial in those halls? How many courts still require witnesses to place their hand on a Bible before giving testimony? Is there a copy of a Qur'an available for Muslims? Could someone simply opt out of placing their hand over a symbol of faith to which they don't agree with or adhere to? How would that influence the jury? Being in the religious minority means you don't have the luxury of avoiding the deliberate presence of the Christian faith.

THE DATING ATHEIST

Then there is the not-so-simple pursuit of creating new relationships, Atheists are no different than anyone else. We need and desire a strong support system as well as companionship. Unfortunately, dating has been a real nightmare for many of us. My frustrations in this category first prompted me to start writing more than two years ago. I'm no different than anyone else. I want to get married, have 2.3 kids, live in a big house with a white picket fence, drive a station wagon and own a big brown dog. You know what I mean.

For just a brief second, I would like to talk about what it's been like trying to find love as a black Atheist. Why the distinction over race? Because African Americans are so entrenched with their religious beliefs that the overwhelming majority of us believe in God literally and completely.

While making connections and building relationships with other black Atheists, the topic of dating and interpersonal relationships seemed to dwarf all others. The emergence of the black Atheist is a very recent event, and its evolution seems to be a very slow process. We make up an extremely small percentage of the total Atheistic population in the states. Most of us live in different areas of the country, and rely solely on the Internet for connection. When I have read blogs about many of their experiences, I shook my head in disbelief, shocked at the statements they received from believers. It makes me wonder if I will ever be able to find a viable candidate for love. Many have told me to simply try and find love outside of my race, claiming that I would never be able to find a black woman that would accept me as an Atheist. While I have no problem with dating interracially, and have done so in my past, I have witnessed a different type of prejudice in that arena. As quietly as it's kept, what percentage of fathers would be overjoyed that their daughter brought a black man to dinner, and an Atheist at that? Because the Black female continues to remain the backbone of the African American church, increasingly and consistently outnumbering men by three or four to one, black male Atheists, like myself, have found it almost impossible to find viable dating options inside our race. By no means does this suggest that the black female Atheist or non-believers of other races have had a walk in the park! Unfortunately the drama that has become commonplace in an effort to find love would put most soap operas to shame, replete with comments such as:

"I would rather date a murderer than an Atheist."

"If you don't believe in God, what's stopping you from trying to kill me right where I stand?"

"I have to get away from you before God decides to judge you. I don't want to be hit by the crossfire."

"I don't want the mother of my children teaching them blasphemy."

"So you're an Atheist, so you must not believe in anything?"

"You're an Atheist; I feel dirty just talking with you!"

"You're an Atheist? Cool. Let's go back to your place and have sex. You must not have any morals."

Understandably, absorbing comments like these have influenced many Atheists to hide their non-belief in hopes of finding realistic options. Some have even suggested pretending to be Christian so they can move forward with their lives, trading their public atheistic stance for a more peaceful everyday life. Living in Atlanta, many of my female friends complain about the fact that some of the guys they meet are gay, but are just on the "Down Low." They hide their homosexual preference so they can lead a normal life, without the fear of ridicule and communal isolation.

In general, this is the same decision facing some Atheists today. Should we hide our true convictions so we can attain a more normal life? Should we place our Atheistic assertions in hibernation until non-belief gains more widespread acceptance? These were some of the initial questions I have resettled with when I first became an Atheist. In the past when someone asked me about church or my faith I opted to simply color the truth.

"I believe in something greater than myself," was the answer I gave to many. Or the ever popular, "I just believe in a higher power." Or any response that would allow me to avoid the "A" word. Now, as a more seasoned Atheist, I simply convey my non-belief and let the chips fall where they may.

The real catalyst that led me to write my story revolved around a relationship I had several years ago. I met a young lady who I will call Monica. During her late teens, Monica considered herself a more radical Christian, but had toned down her aggressive stance in her late 20s. On our third date, we ended up debating morality. Unfortunately she deliberately steeped our conversation in religion. Our discussion quickly turned into a disagreement that knocked on argument's door. Later that night, Monica phoned me, and made it painfully clear that she no longer had an interest in exploring a romantic relationship with me, but that we could still be friends. It was obvious that she had made a judgment about me based on a single conversation. Nevertheless we remained

friends, and as the months went on, our friendship grew quickly.
I helped her with everything from moving into a new home, to
installing appliances, and cleaning her car after it was vandal-
ized. I even babysat her precious rescue dog when I knew I was
allergic. While I felt close to her and really enjoyed our relationship, I never thought she saw me as anything more than the brother
she never had.

That changed one day when we decided to grab a quick bite
to eat. While standing beside her waiting to place our order, she
leaned over and rested her head on my shoulder. While this might
have seemed like a trivial gesture, it was very significant to me,
and I was quite surprised. I pretended to ignore it, but it was the
first time she had shown me any affection in our then six-month-
old friendship. It was also clear her opinion of me had changed.
Later that night, Monica called and confessed she had developed
very real feelings for me and wanted to be more than just friends.
Shocked, I agreed, but was secretly unsure about the change in our
relationship. Unfortunately, I was never given the time to perceive
her in a different light. When we first met, I sensed a real connection to her, and I'm ashamed to admit that I acted like a giddy
schoolboy in her presence. She was the first person that really
made me weak-kneed and gave some credibility to the old adage,
"Love at first sight." But I never let on how disappointed I was the
night she told me she had closed the door on considering me for
anything more than just friendship. On that night I was forced to
face reality and completely dissociate myself from the idea that
she might be the one! I embraced our friendship and pushed the
hope of anything more out of my mind. This was simply the way I
kept platonic relationships with my female friends. While I recognize that I should have explained my apprehension at the time she
confessed feelings for me, I didn't want her to think that I couldn't
love her. If she hadn't judged me on our third date, I would have

never turned the dial to friend mode, adopting a platonic mindset about someone who blew me away on our initial meeting.

That being said, I still chose to push forward with the new relationship. One of the things that really bothered me after we began to date was her attitude. Early on, she admitted that she had the tendency to come off slightly dismissive or even rude on rare occasions. I had seen some markers of this behavior during our friendship, but chose to ignore it. Now that we were more than friends, this conduct gave me real reason for pause. I couldn't understand why someone who claimed to know God's grace and moral principles so well, and had been involved in the faith all her life, struggled with niceties and simple social courtesies that I as an agnostic (at the time) had less difficulty with. Don't get me wrong: she was an amazing person who I grew to love very much, but it's just ironic that the third date conversation on Godly ethics, which made her initially lose interest in me, was a topic that she had far more difficulty with than me. This was especially obvious when we stopped dating. Suddenly I was worthy of contempt, when she was the one who thought we should stop communicating. Even on a few occasions when I bumped into her in public, she ran from me, as if I had routinely abused or beat her during our relationship.

This ultimately hurt me more than she would ever know. I was still very much in love with her, and now I was someone she seemed to fear or loathe! I tried to reach out, even quoting scriptures that outlined forgiveness, but they fell on deaf ears. No matter what I said or did, she ignored me. She simply didn't care how much it hurt me. To me, this just did not seem like the forgiving, Christ-like behavior she had claimed to know so well. At the time I still prayed, and I remember asking God to touch her heart, so we could one day regain the friendship and possibly the relationship that meant so much to me.

Unfortunately, this disappointment turned to real grief, and began to really affect me. In the end this heartbreak made me dwell on faith, religion, and the markers of divinity in believers, and ultimately prompted me to write this book. With that said, I will always love her, and have always wished her nothing but the best. While I know we are now spiritually incompatible, for a time I still held onto the hope that we might one day become friends again. I would even like to thank her, because it was the pain associated with this relationship that led me to write my story.

One afternoon, a friend of mine named Christine and I decided to have lunch at a restaurant called Bahama Breeze. I arrived several minutes ahead of her and decided to be seated, after only a few moments, a really attractive waitress I will call Kim, approached the table. We instantly hit it off and I made my attraction to her obvious. I quickly made lighthearted conversation in an attempt to find more about this young lady who would be filling my sweet teas. She was a hairstylist by day and worked part time waiting tables at night. She had a warm, inviting personality. Clearly interacting with the public was something she did well. She stepped away to attend to a few of her other tables, but with a slight smile said she would be right back.

When she returned to the table, my friend Christine had finally arrived (late as usual) and was sitting across from me. Kim approached the table with a confused look on her face. I know she was asking herself, "Why was this guy openly hitting on me when it looked like he was waiting on a date?" I instantly put her fears to rest and told her that Christine and I were just friends. Relieved, she began to take our orders. I quickly cut her off and asked, "So when do I get to take you out for dinner?"

She smiled and said, "Well, let me see...let's run down my list." Eagerly, she began asking me questions about my background to determine if I was someone she would be interested in getting to know. Judging from the smile on her face, and the fact we had developed such a rapport, I figured I had myself a date as long as my answers weren't crazy. The playful interrogation went something like this:

Kim: So do you have any kids?
Me: No.
Kim: Ever been married?
Me: No.
Kim: Do you have a degree and a job?
Me: Yes and Yes.
Kim: You seem well mannered
Me: I try to be.
Kim: So why in the world are you single?
Me: I just haven't found the right woman yet.
Kim: Oh, OK. Hey, I almost forgot: what church do you attend?

My friend Christine, who had been intently listening to our entire conversation and aware of my Atheistic stance, was visibly disappointed. Not wanting to lie, I told Kim I didn't attend church. With a confused look she asked, "But you do believe in God, right?"

With an apprehensive tone, I told her "No."

This is when everything changed. When she realized I didn't believe in God, not only was I not a viable candidate for a date, I no longer deserved any respect. She instantly looked at me with an annoyed stare and then walked away from the table. Christine said, "It was going so well up until that point!"

I agreed and responded that Kim had given me a look that said, "You know why you're single. If you would erase that chalk pentagram off your basement floor, and stop worshiping that candle-adorned human skull, you might be able to find yourself a girlfriend."

From this point on, our five-star service dropped to a measly half-star. Kim never looked at me the rest of the meal, and only addressed Christine. She even ignored me when I would ask for napkins, more tea or the check.

When it came time to leave, we both needed to-go boxes. Often the wait staff will draw pictures on the lids of carryout containers as a closing touch. I had been to this restaurant several times and was very aware of this practice. I was curious to know what she would draw or write on my box. When she came back to the table and handed us our to-go containers, Christine commented on the attractive beach scene Kim had drawn on her box. Unfortunately, when I looked down at my box, it was completely blank. Shocked, I said to Kim, "I don't get a picture on my box?"

She frowned and drew a circle with two dots for eyes, and a straight line for a mouth. On the way out, I explained to Christine how frustrating it felt to be judged by Christians who are supposed to leave that task to their God. I didn't mind her not being interested in me after finding out we didn't have similar beliefs, but I just couldn't understand the rude treatment. I certainly didn't see any God-like morality in play that evening.

Some time later, I met a very sweet and lovely woman in the bookstore. During our chat, I offered to get her a cup of coffee. She told me she was fasting to get some clarity from God about what should be her next step in life. She proudly stated she was a Christian and began to ask me what church I attended. After explaining I don't believe in organized religion or attend church, I was immediately asked, "But you do believe in God, right?"

I'm always caught off-guard by this question. Obviously, I don't believe in God, as defined by my Atheism, but is this something I want to communicate to everyone I meet? Especially when a conversation is going so well? Is she going to instantly condemn me to hell without even listening to why I've come to such a conclusion? Or will she remain silent, but change her perceptions of me as well as her demeanor?

Reluctantly, I told her I didn't believe in God.

Surprisingly, after explaining I was an Atheist, she was not shocked, and was still willing to continue our conversation. She asked if I had simply belonged to the wrong church as a possible reason for my conversation. I explained that I have yet to find a church that can answer my questions or provide the evidence I was looking for. Seeing this as a rare opportunity to talk about faith with someone who was very open minded, I asked why she believed in Christianity and not any other system of belief.

"The evidence made me believe," she confidently said.

Evidence? I instantly perked up, wanting to know more about this evidence. She went on to say Jesus was a real man, and people saw the empty tomb. I had heard this type of "proof" before, but of course, words in a book or an empty tomb are not evidence of a deity in human form or a divine resurrection. Many scholars might argue whether Jesus was a real figure or not, but that certainly does not mean he was a messiah or could perform miracles. In fact both Islam and Judaism claim that Jesus was not the savior and that this divine character has yet to appear!

After I pointed this out, she acknowledged that it was a matter of faith, and that she believed in Jesus because it was taught to her as a child. We talked about several other topics, but to make a long story short, I really enjoyed the opportunity to have intelligent, respectful religious debate. The one trait that set her apart from so many others was her willingness to say, "I don't know," when asked questions she could not answer. She was also someone that actively pursued questions until she satisfied her curiosity. Whether or not she remained a theist or made the move toward non-belief, I respected her confident demeanor and mature pursuit for answers.

One day, I got off the phone with one of my close friends. She's married with three beautiful children and really loves the Lord. Unfortunately, she hasn't the faintest idea that I no longer consider myself a Christian. Many years ago, I routinely visited her church and participated in several ministries, so it's no fault of hers that she's not aware of my conversion. She's also someone I don't want to lose from my life, although I understand that it might be a very real possibility when she finds out about my choice. I really enjoy our friendship and her family, but like so many Atheists, I'm afraid of what her reaction will be.

This trepidation and uneasiness was a learned behavior. It developed after witnessing several extreme responses from other professed friends when they learned I was no longer a believer. It's astonishing how a single deceleration can completely change how you're perceived. Many people have instantly expected adverse changes in my behavior after finding out I'm an Atheist, not realizing that I had been a non-believer long before it was ever brought to their attention.

Suddenly I'm not to be trusted, even when I supported you during church services, babysat your children, and watched your homes and pets while you were away on vacation. Now everything I said was a lie, even when you have never known me to be dishonest or deceptive! Effortlessly forgetting that you once told me my integrity was one of my greatest qualities, often leading you and others to seek my honest advice. I'm still the same person who helped you move when everyone else bailed; picked you up from the airport when you were stranded; spent time with you when you were lonely; lent you the money to pay your mortgage, even when I had my own burdens; rescued your drunk self from a late night party, being sure you made it home safely; or gave you the concerned shoulder to cry on when the bad boy you've been dating acted like a fool for the millionth time! I don't know why you feel like things need to change between us, because I still love you! Your privileged place in my life will never be altered because of my personal choice. I'm not broken or lost, and this is not a cry for help or guidance. So please don't trick me into meeting a minister or spiritual counselor. You've done far more than scratched the surface of who I am, so stop judging this very familiar book by its Atheistic cover. Just accept me for the person I have become and reject the selfish notion of what you think I should still be. This is all I ever wanted, the reciprocated love, respect and understanding that I have always shown towards you and yours.

This is essentially what I'm looking for: not to be judged based on a single conversation or assertion. While I have no issue with someone choosing not to pursue a relationship with me based on differing core beliefs, I am frustrated with being berated for a single declaration of non-belief, quickly followed by continual attempts at conversion. Out of respect for someone's faith, I have never tried to convince anyone to leave his or her religion. I just wish this respect were mutual! I'm tired of someone feeling like they need to change or belittle me for my personal choices. I think this arrogant assertion is what galvanizes Atheists to stand against religion in a more, in-your-face fashion, rather than trying to soften hearts in an attempt to gain simple acceptance.

WHAT'S WRONG WITH ATHEISM?

"Stop attacking us!" Is the plea made by many in our camp as we put the finishing touches on our nativity display with the heading, "He never really existed!"

"You Christians are deluded. Why in the world do you believe any of that nonsense?" arrogantly says the former believer pretending to have forgotten their own weary wayward walk of absolute certainty.

"Please Please Please…bring up religion so I can crush you in a debate," was the only secular prayer made by the fledgling Atheist that wanted to flaunt his new knowledge and non-belief. Figuring they had to go on the offensive and become that squeaky wheel if they were ever going to get respect.

"You need to control those Christian crazies," one said, while almost purposely turning a blind eye to the unbalanced Atheists in our midst who might one day give rise to extremism or funda-mentalism in our own group, and whose acts would surely be held against all non-believers.

"You need to figure it out on your own… I did!" Was the non-chalant response given to the believer we finally convinced to

consider and embrace our perspective! We quickly dismiss our responsibilities as Atheistic tour guide or counselor to this new freethinker we helped create.

"But I never believed" is the mantra of some, almost offered as the reason for their blatant disregard for theistic belief, which has undoubtedly led to their dismissive and cavalier attitude towards the faith of the everyday kind-hearted believer?

"Come out, come out wherever you are!" is the battle cry from our fellow Atheists, easily ignoring the extreme consequences for some after making such a public assertion, often shaming many nonbelievers into stepping onto the front line of this debate, assuredly forcing some to become casualties in this conflict.

"Stand up and be counted, no matter what the consequences" was the singular mindset from some Atheists, not realizing that their publicly dehumanizing rejection might do more harm than good, forcing the quietly skeptical onlookers to think twice about taking similar steps towards non-belief.

"But I want change now" say the impatient few, wanting to transform the world overnight, seemingly unwilling to take one for the team so future generations of Atheists could benefit from their due diligence.

While I agree the above represents the vast minority of us, comments like these are the ones remembered, quoted, and given airtime in social circles, discussed in Chat rooms, posted on Facebook, or continually showing up in religious tweets!

We challenge the passers-by to a debate about their faith, not by any formal declaration or prearranged meeting, but by our dismissive responses when we are told to have a blessed day or a reference is made to God being good, easily ignoring the stranger's genuine gesture of kindness.

"Now's my chance to put another religious nut in their place, and win another skirmish in the battle for Atheism," thought the veteran and amateur Atheist alike. But what is that going to prove? Do you really think he or she is going to run back to their local church and tell the tale of how you were more knowledgeable or logical than they were, going on to admit they now have some real food for thought and are seriously doubting their faith? Or will they simply explain how you came off as pompous jerk, disgusting them with your aggressively dismissive tone during the entire conversation? Giving their audience something to rally behind, fueling their distrust of us and changing the way they deal with every non-believer in the future? Am I saying you should take one under the chin when someone is attacking you?

Of course not! However, you have to keep in mind that this is not a hobby for them, or something they do to pass the time. They truly believe God is communicating with them in subtle ways, and are sincerely trying to discern and obey his will. They fear hell as a very real place where people are tortured for eternity! To them it's a part of who they are, and by dismissing God, you're dismissing them. So that means they can't stand idly by while you question their faith, without trying to defend it. So stop acting surprised when you get a strong reaction from someone after you told them they were crazy for believing in God. How can we convince others to be tolerant of our non-belief by being intolerant of their beliefs?

This issue of acceptance has been my goal since I began to write my story. In that time, I have latched onto other non-believers for support. Unfortunately, I have been witness to some extreme dogmatism in this group, which has really bothered me. I sometimes feel the arrogance of some in our position can on occasion result in a very dismissive attitude towards faith. Don't get me wrong: it's a small percentage of us, and I understand the frustration of being told you're going to hell by someone who doesn't even know you; or being tired of the "I just have faith" answers when you have tried to completely explain yourself, freely admitting when you didn't know something. But we must remain cordial to keep the lines of communication open. In my opinion, any group that doesn't carefully police itself and refuses to denounce poor behavior by its members, could eventually produce an extremist or fundamentalist sect. I personally think this also includes Atheism. While we have not claimed responsibility for the bombing of a fundamentalist or extremist church, murder of a child molesting pastor, or even the defacing of a religious billboard, it's only a matter of time before some crazy non-believer takes extreme action to try and make an equally extreme point.

We must keep in mind that anyone that has ever been reached and converted to non-belief never did so through aggressively demeaning rants. Don't get me wrong, I struggle with patience as much as the next person, probably more so. But I firmly believe it's the only way to facilitate acceptance or even change. Think about it. Anyone you have been able to connect with was probably a loved one, a family member, close friend, significant other or co-worker. Your shared emotional bond mated to your caringly kind influence allowed them to genuinely consider what you had to say. I'm not saying your careful study and reasoned answers didn't make a difference, but without them knowing you and having a vested interest in the relationship, they would have never been open to listening to you in the first place.

The most important thing we all need to remember is that it took time; it rarely ever happens overnight! They weren't considering agnosticism or Atheism in the first conversation. Remember, we were once where they were. Only through confusion, wishful faith-affirming investigation, thought provoking conversation, and conceded realization about faith did we arrive at non-belief.

However, if someone had forcibly pushed a hostile, "there is no God" agenda in your face, you would have rejected it also!

You also would have rejected our position if you felt like many were openly trying to dishonor your long-standing customs or rituals. Personally I'm not a fan of attacking a particular holiday of any belief system. I am often criticized for this perspective, but I just don't understand why we need to denounce Christmas as though it were the issue in-and-of itself. I personally enjoy the holiday season, especially the music. I just don't believe in the religious sentiments, although I realize that it's the reason for the celebration. However, I'm all for the messages of neighborly love, or that it's better to give than to receive, etc. I like the gathering of family and atmosphere of goodwill, although I could do without the commercialization. But I will always defend someone's right to believe and celebrate as they wish, as long as it's not harming or affecting others.

Some Atheists say to me, "Yes, I worship science and am proud of it, because I now require solid evidence for everything in my life or it just doesn't exist. I will no longer use the word 'supernatural' to explain the unexplainable." To them, this was the stamp of the ignorant and ridiculous. So now they have made a complete about-face, assuredly claiming that anything failing to meet their personal criteria for sufficient evidence didn't exist and never would. Easily ignoring the blanket statement they have just placed over all phenomena, effortlessly casting anything strange or mysterious into the category of mythology, they are quick to overlook their own ignorance on a particular subject, along with the genuine scientific research being done all across the globe. Their failures to acknowledge areas in need of further study could one-day subject them to disappointment and ridicule if science proves the existence of phenomena they've passed off as fantasy. Many of our civilization's greatest advancements began as wild ideas and unsupported guesses about the unexplained. The only difference is science impartially looks for answers, and theism imparts God on the questions. Science validates a speculation with evidence, and religion validates an assertion by faith.

One of my biggest concerns is this ease at which an Atheist tries to walk away after successfully persuading someone to doubt or critically examine their faith. Too often, their attitude is "Onto the next!" with little regard for the inner battle waging in the skeptic they helped create. Remember, when you're asking someone to reject the notion of a God, while trying to instill the idea that they shouldn't believe in anything without evidence, you are removing something at the same time. What are you replacing their faith with? As they see it, their God has pulled them through every issue they have ever encountered, with phrases like "Let go and let God" remaining constant mantras for the faithful. So it's not surprising that they have come to rely on this sense of security created by faith. By emotionally sharing the hardships in life with their God, they feel some relief, and this affect is very tangible and well documented. Now we're telling them to simply go at it alone. We must avoid pulling the safety net out from under them and then refuse to help them through the sometimes arduous process of finding more tangible coping mechanisms.

So try and see it from their perspective, and be patient.

Another previously mentioned area of concern is the complexity at which Atheism is presented. We don't do a very good job of emotionally connecting with our opposition, choosing to only present a very intellectually stale message, often void of feelings, other than frustration of course!

When I read Christian literature, it was far more simplistic. The authors made their points using layman's vocabulary and pulling on the reader's emotions. They seemed to know their audience well and write in much the same way a pasture preaches.

In "*A Case for Faith*," Lee Strobel does a good job of pulling in the reader with personal accounts of why many believe in, and love the Lord. He expertly mirrored the thoughts and feelings of the everyday Christian. While I did not agree with its conclusions, I felt like I wanted to! However, when I read the Atheistic literature, it was filled with facts, not feelings, and packed with brilliant, but sometimes intellectually exclusive material. While I agreed with their messages, they didn't make the same emotional connection with me. Even though all of the information was backed by independently verifiable facts, it felt more like I was reading a graduate level textbook written by a witty educated scholar. Wow, that actually sounded really critical, and that was not my intention. I loved the literature put out by some of the popular Atheist authors. I just hoped the narrative would be delivered in a more conversational language, utilizing terms familiar to the vast majority of the populace and used on a daily basis. I wanted to recommend the books to people of any educational background. I also was hoping to hear a small amount of empathy for religious belief, as well as the inner turmoil in making the transition to Atheism. If the goal is social and political acceptance from the theistic masses, we must make a connection with its constituents. To do so, we need to show the transparent, emotional, compassionate side of Atheism.

When I hear people talk about their switch to Atheism they merely explain how the religious claims never made any sense to them. After researching the information for themselves, they came to the conclusion that God didn't exist. But from my point of view, they failed to expand on the private struggle behind their conversion, rarely detailing how hard it was to leave a faith they had come to count on and believe in all their lives. Or about the times they found themselves calling out to God, even when they were pretty sure he didn't exist: "OK, God, if you're really out there and want me to renew my faith in you, I need your intervention now."

Even when they felt comfortable with their new journey, they still had feelings about blatantly denouncing God's name. I feel like people need to see how difficult the decision was for some of us, and the inner turmoil we experienced, showing others that we aren't simply standing on our self-appointed intellectual soap-boxes, purposely speaking above their heads, as though we had never walked in their shoes. The everyday believer needs to see the compassion for their faith and theistic belief from our side of the argument. When you go to church, the pastor is very moving and animated, showing empathy, love, compassion, and synthetic confusion before conveying their poignant message. This is what draws people in and allows them to completely identify with their church leaders, sincerely believing their claims, which in turn validates their reason for faith. This was certainly how I felt when I was involved in Christianity.

I didn't start down an Atheistic path because of what a 14th century thinker said, the genetic evidence in our DNA linking us to primates, or the conflicting ideologies of cultures on the other side of the globe. What made me start doubting my faith was the fact that its most basic claims could not be verified. I never could accept the Garden of Eden story as fact, simply because it was never presented with any supporting evidence. I couldn't under-stand why the Bible was considered the word of God, when it was not written by him, but by men, and there were so many other alleged divine doctrines, not solely because it often violated scien-tific norms and theories. I couldn't understand why I was supposed to say, "God did it," every time something good happened in my life. Not because I didn't understand the intricacies of quantum mechanics. I couldn't understand why morality was impossible without God when I had been doing fine on my own, long before

I ever believed in him. Not because similar but primitive systems of right and wrong were present for many thousands of years while man evolved from early hominids to Bronze Age *homo sapiens*. I couldn't understand why I had to give money to the church, when I thought God should be able to provide for his anointed preachers and prophets, not because of the statistics outlining the number of religious scams being perpetrated all across the globe.

While the intellectual discourse and factual information ultimately helped me solidify, defend and explain my Atheism, it was not the catalyst. We are not Vulcans or Androids (both void of emotion). So the Atheistic community needs to figure out the same thing that religious leaders have known since antiquity. Faith is fueled by belief, and beliefs are created and sustained more by emotions and feelings than logic or intellect. When was the last time you were baffled by the pastor's message? Probably not often, because the pastor understands the importance of preaching a message that can be easily understood by the entire congregation. I sometimes think Atheists stop conversations before they begin by purposely trying to intellectually distance someone from the discussion. Often, they flaunt the knowledge they gain from their study of the sciences and literature written by leading Atheistic authors. Unfortunately, by their very nature, the theist will purposely leave certain questions unasked in lieu of faith!

That being said, I freely admit that the most popular Atheistic literature, whose narrative has become the backbone for the movement, would not have been given the same merit if void of certain language and written by un-credentialed authors. This began to explain the intellectual overtone during formal religious discourse. There was almost a conscious effort to impress and come off as learned and cerebral, seemingly to justify why someone is considered an expert and deserves to be standing behind the podium representing their entire ideology in this setting. I further embraced this notion when I noticed the stark contrast when the Atheist or theist gave an informal talk, or was interviewed in a more casual setting. In those contexts, they seemed to do a much better job of coming off more down to earth and reaching all audiences, not only those with an advanced vocabulary and high intellectual prowess.

Don't get me wrong. I completely understand that religion is a faith-based system, and therefore is not going to rely heavily on scientific data, and for many non-believers it was the science that influenced many of them to finally, although not initially, start down the path of Atheism. But one of the differences for me between the Atheists and theists, facts and feelings, was in the use of language:

The theist says, "Abandoning the faith." The Atheist says, "Apostasy."

The theist says, "Free will doesn't exist." The Atheist says, "Hard determinism."

The theist talks about "moral beliefs being different in other cultures." The Atheist says, "Moral relativism"

The theist says, "A culture with many Gods." The Atheist says, "Polytheism."

The theist says, "I'm trying to figure out where everything came from in our Universe." The Atheist says, "I'm studying the cosmological model."

On a larger scale, the theist says he or she believes in God because it helps them deal with everyday issues. The Atheist simply says, "You're delusional," then proceeds to discuss the neurology of the human brain, rarely offering to walk the believer through alternative methods of managing life's stresses. The theist claims he has the answer to man's most plaguing question of where everything came from, but the Atheist replies, "I don't know, and no one does," going on to explain string theory, M theory, and the multiverse, rarely outline why it's okay not to know, or the beauty in someday uncovering the real answers.

Since knowledge is power, do you really think that in the midst of a disagreement someone is going to relinquish some of theirs by admitting they haven't the foggiest idea of what you're talking about? The only point I'm trying to make is that we need to show flexibility. We can still say the same things, just more simplistically, more compassionately, and hopefully connect with more people. If we really are trying to reach the masses, I think we need to do a better job in acknowledging the emotional component of religion and faith, and not just dismissing it, while at the same time using language and concepts that are easily understood by everyone. While I'm in complete agreement that some ideas and theories are complex by their very nature, we need to take a cue from educators in every discipline that have been successfully conveying complex ideas in our school systems for centuries.

So I would love to see bookshelves on Atheism (when not confined to the philosophy section) lined with the personal stories of people rejecting their indoctrinated faith. Passionately explaining how difficult it was to abandon their religious belief, and how it affected every facet of their lives, in a manner that resonates with everyone. When I was in my conversion process, I really wanted to hear from other Atheists about the difficulties and emotions associated with the transition. I just wanted know and feel like I wasn't alone, and more importantly, not crazy. I knew the fact and figures, but I needed to feel like I wasn't the only one that struggled with the symptoms of religious withdrawal.

HELPING THE CAUSE

When I first became an Atheist, I wanted to know what I could do to help the movement, and I also thought it would be in my best interest to help others answer this question. Unfortunately, I can only pass along some of the ideas I have heard from others, along with the few things that have worked for me. So this is the only limited advice I can give Atheists who want to know what they can do to help the cause.

First and foremost, be comfortable with your decision. If you're still on the fence, or aren't completely sure about your stance on this issue of belief, I encourage you to continue searching for answers. At the end of the day, if you decide theistic belief is something to which you want to return, you can do so with the confidence that you honestly sought answers to validate your beliefs, and your choice to return to your faith was an informed one. However, if you decide that Atheism is the right choice for you, then I guess it would be time to decide what is going to be your stance. I know that sounds a little odd, but I simply mean what will this statement of non-belief mean to you?

My stance has evolved over the past several years, and I have met many Atheists with varied perspectives on what their

assertion means to them. The private Atheist seemed to be someone looking to have as little disruption to his or her daily life as
possible, willing to go along with most of the religious rhetoric
to keep the peace, or lower their head in prayer when amongst
believers. He or she might nod in agreement when religious assertions are made, or a reference is made to God affecting someone's circumstance, voluntarily attend religious services to fill a
communal or family obligation, vehemently avoid questions about
their beliefs, and who aren't interested in debating their decision
with others if their non-belief is discovered. It's a completely
private decision that they prefer to keep to themselves.

I also ran into passive Atheists, who are fine with their affirmation that there isn't a God, and the title of Atheism, but don't think
it's the right choice for everyone. Deciding if someone needs to
believe in a God to get through the day, or keep them from acting
immoral, then its fine with them as long as they are not trying to
change their beliefs or legislate their faith on others. They might
respectively bow their heads when meals are blessed in their presence, but maybe are less likely to agree when a religious assertion
is made. They are mildly willing to discuss and/or defend their
decision if warranted, but they are not looking for a fight or debate.
Some close friends might know about their decision, but it's not
common knowledge. They have believers as friends without trying
to challenge their faith, and who might attend services when asked.

The moderate Atheists seemed happy with their decisions.
Most, if not all, of their friends and family are aware of their choice.
They might be involved in helping others make the transition, and
in the movement itself. They might be comfortably versed in the
arguments, but doesn't necessarily search for opportunities to debate. However, on most occasions, they won't avoid the discussion either. They are willing to calmly educate anyone about their
perspective and clear up any misconceptions. They might attend

conferences or investigate both sides of the argument, further educating themselves with Atheistic and religious cultures alike.

Then there was the hard-line Atheist, someone who is not only comfortable with the title of Atheism, but can't understand why anyone in the absence of evidence believes differently. They are very accustomed to, and comfortable with, arguing their position. They are actively involved in the movement, even if it only means aggressively debating everyone they come across. They are not willing to go-with-the religious flow to keep the peace, but will vehemently defend Atheism, possibly in a more dogmatic fashion. They are far less likely to let an opportunity pass to educate the masses.

Obviously these are just my personal observations, and most Atheists are a combination of these viewpoints. My own Atheistic stance is a collection of these ideas. However, I feel very strongly about not becoming the very thing we are so passionately opposing. We can never use fear and intimidation to force others to our way of thinking. Yelling or threatening someone with physical harm, or the use of material or social blackmail (in my opinion) must be avoided at all costs. Intolerant rants made in public settings would seem to be the most damaging. Who would want to associate themselves with Atheism, or any form of belief or non-belief, if it appeared to be as divisive or authoritarian as the system it's condemning for the very same reasons? While I completely understand that 2+2 = 4, regardless of the demeanor of the person making the argument, and that the information should be assessed on its merit alone, and not on someone's feelings about the person making the claim, I just don't think that's the world we live in. Unfortunately, many people are guided more by their emotions than the validity of an opposing argument. So we need to claim the moral high ground and remain calm in the face of heated debates, and let the religious lose their cool and defy their supposed superior morality. I also personally never try to make claims that are not supported by the same reason and logic that I require of the religious systems of faith. I won't allege my dead ancestors are guiding me, when it can't be substantiated. I don't state that the great equalizing force of the Universe will take care of me, if I can't prove it. Otherwise, the deity of my opposition could just as easily exist in the same place as my unfounded claims exist.

One of the most important things that helped me find answers for others was to know my material. Inevitably, you're going to be questioned about your non-belief. Having logical, well thought-out answers will be important for the opposition and inquisitive alike. You don't need to become a scientist, theologian or a philosopher, but you do need to offer basic responses that confirm and support your position and decision. Showing others that you came to your choice through detailed unbiased research, and not because you just wanted to sin. Most importantly, you should always exemplify patience when engaged in sensitive, although important discourse.

Be smart. Martyrs can be just as damaging as they are heroic. If you live in a small town or area where fundamentalist ideologies are at their strongest, making a socially suicidal Atheistic deceleration will only make your public rejection and societal isolation a position to be feared and avoided at all costs. Such an approach would only cause the secret skeptics in your area to further retreat into the communal sanctuary of religious faith. So I would persuade you to go online and find others in your area that share your beliefs. Make discreet connections while continuing to learn more about what's happening across the country. Create local groups, so you can vent about your religious frustrations, while organizing strategies to gain acceptance in your community. Even a group of two can provide mutual emotional support while the rest of the movement continues to win small battles of acceptance across the country.

However, never undervalue the importance of day-to-day encounters that can go a long way to slowly changing the minds of many. Again I'm looking for acceptance from others, not necessarily conversion. In my experience the people with whom I have had the strongest connections were the ones willing to hear my argument. Start educating your family members and close friends in a casual, non-confrontational manner. Point out inconsistencies with their thought processes, religious messages and alleged divine interventions, but do it kindly. Eventually we will, as Richard Dawkins once said in a conference, reach critical mass, where being ignored will not be an option and we can hopefully enjoy some of the same freedoms as other formally ostracized groups.

Like every oppressed group, the first step on the front line of social change can become martyrs for the cause. African Americans like myself enjoy many equalities and freedoms as a direct result of the sacrifices made by the men and women who first dared to say no: "No, I'm not going to sit in the back of the bus;" "No, I'm not leaving the counter of this white diner;" "No, I don't believe blacks are inferior just because our ancestors once enslaved them." Unfortunately, they sometimes paid the ultimate price for their brazen resistance. It takes a very special individual, who will stand alone for what he or she believes in, in the face of vehement opposition, no matter the cost. I'm sure there are people that identify with my story, and even in the black community. But, being the first to step out alone, opposing years of indoctrination, is far more than some are willing to do.

During the past ten years, Atheism and agnosticism have grown at an impressive pace. I personally believe this only reflects the number of people that secretly doubted their beliefs, and finally found the courage to state it publicly. Don't get me wrong, the number of people in doubt may be a small minority, and the religious majority will simply dismiss my argument and assume hell has a very special place for me. That's fine—I'm not trying to change anyone's mind. But for those that have a smidgen of doubt. I encourage you to seek answers for your questions privately. In the 21st century, answers are only a click away.

Several decades ago, if you questioned your religious teachings, you would likely feel isolated and ashamed. You would probably be left to assume that everyone else was a devout believer with no real doubts about their faith. You would find a quiet corner in your local library and research your questions in an attempt to find much needed answers, desperately hoping that no one you knew would discover your wavering faith or intentions. Nowadays, we have the internet, email, chat rooms, Facebook and Youtube. If the new generation has any doubt about a particular belief, they can simply google it, chat with people on the other side of the globe, or watch video opinions on a multitude of web sites. Instantly you realize you're not alone, and that your questions have been asked a countless number of times. The Atheism vs. Theism debate has raged for thousands of years. In the past decade or so, we have seen a real emergence of non-belief, agnosticism, Atheism, freethinkers, humanists, etc.

Some have compared this emergence process of culturally unpopular ideas to the gay and lesbian movement that started decades ago and is now more accepted. It's not to say that the community doesn't have a long way to go, but you certainly see more homosexual imagery in mainstream culture today than say…20 years ago. Atheism may be a long way from that level of freedom. But the only way we will reach that initial plateau of acceptance is if the doubters become discernible from the devout.

PART FIVE:

Random Thoughts

THE BRAINWASHED BELIEVER

Now that I'm a non-believer, I have often contemplated why I accepted the idea of religious faith so completely. Today, I can say with some certainty that its hold was directly related to how I interpreted and perceived everything associated with my faith. I touched on this earlier, but I cannot overstress the importance of this psychological construct. If faith is the engine that propels you down a alleged divinely inspired path, then your personal interpretation of your experiences, mated to your social environment, is the fuel that sustains that engines ever-increasing forward momentum. This is by far the most difficult idea for me to grasp and explain.

I also believe that this is one of the greatest gaps in understanding between Atheists and Theists. Atheists require tangible, testable, predictable evidence. Theists believe through faith; their need for tangible evidence is satisfied by their alleged personal experiences with God. The predictable and testable nature of their beliefs is associated with and confirmed by their own interpretations of those experiences. OK, let me try to be clearer. The devoutly religious often believe experiences like finding a job, surviving hard times, birth, life and death are all examples of

God's will in action. By associating the good with God and ignoring or labeling the bad as something else, God's will appears to be
very consistent. The problem for non-believers enters when that
experience is set against similar circumstances, and critical questions go unasked and unanswered.

Think back to a time in your life when you felt God showed
you favor and unequivocally blessed you. The problem for non-
believers is centered on the unasked questions that would authenticate the claim: Is your experience only shared by members of
your faith? If not, why would God bless non-believers? What evidence do you have of God's involvement? Did you take any action to affect the outcome? Are you simply observing one event in
isolation, or are you comparing all events surrounding a given idea
and goal and making an objective answer based on the numbers?
Once asked, non-believers often receive answers like, "I just have
faith", "I just know," etc. This is the point where we find it more
difficult to accept the initial claim of Godly intervention. Often,
we suspect that many of these supposed divine events are given
credence without meeting any criteria. For me, this was the heart
of the issue. Are miracles, or blessings from God, required to meet
any standard before they can be stamped 100% All-God?

The Atheist finds it hard to accept the idea that there's a hid-
den meaning or intelligence behind every event in our lives. The
concept of Karma and proverbs like "Good things come to those
who wait", "Everything happens for a reason," or "Every cloud
has a silver lining" were all ideas, like religion, without quantifi-
able or measurable evidence. Additionally, when dealing with believers, we found that coincidence, chance or random events were
rejected notions when cited in a religious context. Your whole life
you have been taught everything happens for a reason. There is
no luck, just fate. This was a powerful tool in setting up the psychological constructs used to perceive the demonstrable will of

God. By not believing in luck or random events, it forces you to find meaning in every circumstance. If you break a heel before going on a date, God must be telling you this is not the right guy for you, or the Devil is trying to keep you from your future husband. If you're stuck in a traffic jam on the way to your doctor's office, God wants you to put your faith in him, or the Devil is trying to keep you from feeling better. By simply implanting the idea that every circumstance is potentially an example of divine guidance, you artificially create significance behind otherwise arbitrary events.

Ironically, Karma has origins in the Hindu religion of India. So it's not surprising that this idea has been adopted by other cultures to control behavior. Like many things that are commandeered by the West, it has been simplified by our culture and void of its initial meaning or intentions. Many Americans believe that Karma is the great equalizer of the Universe. Its construct assures that the righteous will be ultimately rewarded for their good deeds, and the wicked will be punished for their transgressions. Like miracles, Karma is not required to meet any qualifiers. You are simply expected to believe he or she will get theirs in the end. Obviously, most of us will have something negative or positive occur in our lives if enough time passes. This would qualify as meeting the requirement of Karma. The vast majority of us are not guilty of any truly heinous acts, or Nobel peace prize worthy kindness. So in the cases of extreme good and evil, Karma can only be fulfilled in the afterlife. For example, there were many former Nazi concentration camp war criminals that escaped justice and lived reasonably pleasant lives under false identities. Believers in Karma would simply claim ignorance about their circumstances and assert they will be punished in hell. Similar assertions would be made about babies being crushed in earthquakes or drowning in tsunamis. They will receive peace and blessing in the afterlife.

Belief in Karma is just a way people try to explain why bad things happen to good people and vice-versa.

The same idea applies to God's will. Unfortunately, it's completely up to the *individual* to determine the level of divine involvement. For example, a friend of mine, we will call Tracey, phoned me late one afternoon very disturbed by the conversation she just had with a close girlfriend. Apparently her friend and co-worker, Jane, was desperately trying to find a clinic in her area that would terminate her pregnancy for $225. Unfortunately for her, the lowest price she could find was $350. Wanting the procedure to be completed immediately, she arrived at the cheapest local clinic she could find in hopes of pleading with the staff to perform the surgery at a lower cost. She was astonished to find out the price had just been lowered to $225, the exact amount she had in her wallet! Overjoyed, Jane immediately called Tracey to convey the good news. "God was certainly on my side today," she said. "He always meets my needs. He knew exactly what I could spend and made it work. This is no coincidence; I just give him all the glory and praise."

Tracey simply sat in bewilderment, never letting on how appalled she was by the claim that this abortion was a blessing from God. She quickly ended the conversation, and immediately called me. After explaining the whole story, she instantly expressed her disgust at how effortlessly her friend attached her heavenly father to what she considered a despicable act.

Remember when I spoke about my brother leaving his job at the Twin Towers about a year or two before the attacks, a coincidence that was not divine favor but just a product of circumstance? I remember hearing about another 9/11 story. A woman who was inside one of the towers during the attack, sadly she was the only member of her group to make it out alive. When interviewed, she instantly proclaimed she was saved by God's grace, and he must have some unfulfilled purpose for her life. For many, I think this assertion would be accepted without question. Personally, I would have been interested to know why she thought her life was more valuable than the others who died in the tragedy. Why did she have more purpose, or unfinished business, than say...the children that were killed? Was she a more devout Christian than the other believers that perished?

Which of these stories would be considered a true blessing from God? Who has the right to determine what can be categorized as a miracle or an example of Godly favor? Without any criteria, any event meeting your personal idea of divine intervention can be considered an example of his will for your life, completely reinforcing your belief in prayer and faith. Many will claim that God's love allows him to bless the believer and non-believer alike, and I would certainly accept this line of thinking if there were any observable or discernable pattern, anything that would suggest a sentient intelligence at work. But, of course, this is not the case.

Religion is taught at a very early age. Studies show that children introduced to religious principles are far more likely to carry these ideas well into adulthood. In *The God Delusion*, Richard Dawkins considers indoctrinating children to religion a form of child abuse. While I know these are very strong words, I understand his intention. He's simply trying to illustrate how susceptible and impressionable children's minds are, and insisting they aren't being given the opportunity to make an informed, uninfluenced decision later in life. As unpopular as it sounds, God is no different from fairy tales we tell children about the Easter Bunny, Santa Claus or the tooth fairy. I would even argue if given the right circumstances, we could get a child to believe these fairy-tales well into adulthood. With this philosophy in mind, we could influence any child to grow up and believe almost anything we wanted them to.

As a society, we have determined which claims require evidence and which don't. If I said, "I saw aliens in my morning toast," I would instantly be called crazy. But if the bread contained a picture of the Virgin Mary, I would have people camped outside my door for weeks. When your parents openly talk about someone going to hell, they are making it painfully clear how they feel about the subject. Children internalize these fears and amplify them as they enter adulthood. As we stated before, no matter where you are born, an overwhelming percent of the population's children believe as their society does. So if you were born in Afghanistan, you would believe in Allah. If you were born in ancient Greece, you might believe in Zeus. If you were born in America, you would statistically believe in the Christian God. The point is there is no singularly recognized, specific God that is apparent to all humanity, regardless of where you were born. Someone who has never heard of the Christian God, because of his or her remote location, would have to be taught this ideology. They wouldn't receive some divine impression that would teach them the Christian principles through some kind of heavenly osmosis. Furthermore, according to that same system of belief (set up by the deity), they would be doomed to hell, simply because they weren't fortunate enough to have been born in a specific area where the alleged one true religion is being practiced.

To me, this is ridiculous, and for those who say God won't return until his word is taught in all four corners of the world. That probably won't mean much to the multitude of past generations doomed to a fiery hell because they were born in the wrong place or at the wrong time. Ask yourself, are you perfectly fine with serving a God that clearly states in his word, none will find salvation but through my son Jesus Christ, and would quickly send someone to hell for eternity, even if they had no way of knowing their alleged predicament?

Remember when I talked about Christians explaining to me
that God blesses the believer and non-believer? I personally think
this idea was only suggested after it was made very apparent that
the claims of blessings made by believers were continually dupli-
cated in the lives of non-believers, and people of differing faiths.
The church needed an explanation for this. But of course this gen-
erosity of equal blessings doesn't apply to life after death, simply
because the conditions that exist beyond death are unknown to us.
This argument from ignorance will never be considered evidence.
But unfortunately it's continually flaunted in one form or another
for the existence of God, the Devil, heaven and hell.

Sometimes, children believe monsters live in their closets or
under their beds, and are afraid of the dark or being alone. They
truly believe that some strange creature will grab them when their
parents turn off the lights and say good night. So as parents, you
explain to them that there are no such things as monsters, showing them that the figure seen in the corner of the dark room was
just a football helmet hanging from a chair covered by a pair of
old socks. You carefully filter what television programs and media they watch, because their minds can't process the images in
certain films and are slaves to their self-created mental imagery.

Given this common occurrence in households across America, why is it so hard to believe or admit that your beliefs were
undeniably affected when your parents read or told stories about
Noah's Ark, Moses, or the Garden of Eden? Or rousted you out of
bed every Sunday for church? Or incessantly forced you to read
the Bible or pray before meals? Or made continuous references to
God blessing your family because your father landed a new job,
your sister won her dance competition, or your mother's blood
pressure came down? You're lucky to have any doubt at all.

This conditioning is the foundation for religion, and why
its hold is so absolute. Strong belief indoctrinated at an early

age, coupled with a flawed psychological construct and continual communal reinforcement, leads to religious permanence. The words "flawed psychological construct" might simply be stated as "brainwashing," which is defined as: "Controlled systematic indoctrination based on repetition or confusion: A method for systematically changing attitudes or altering beliefs, through the use of torture, drugs or psychological-stress techniques, in which the planted ideas are taught not to be questioned."

I'm not trying to be rude, although I realize that claiming billions of people have been brainwashed is not a great start. I will simply blame my limited imagination for not coming up with a better example. Nevertheless, the part that I find most interesting about this definition refers to the systematic changing of attitudes, psychological-stress techniques in which the planted ideas were taught not to be questioned.

"But I'm an adult, not some naive child who simply believes what they are told. My mind is my own, and can't be illogically frightened or brainwashed," says many a believer. Fine, but have you ever been to a movie that was able to illicit an illogical response? For instance, I had many friends watch a movie called *Paranormal Activity*. After leaving the theatre, they were terrified, and unable to sleep for several days. They swore they constantly heard strange noises in their bedrooms, or thought they saw something in the dark. Why did they feel this way? How could they be scared of something that they knew wasn't real? How could they be tricked into believing in monsters when, before the movie, they would have laughed at the idea?

It's because our minds are not much different from when we were children and our imaginations are simply getting the best of us. The brain has an amazing power to generate perceptions of all kinds. The only reason these responses of fear or sadness from watching a movie don't linger for more than a few hours or days is because they are not reinforced. You don't continually subject yourself to mind-altering events consistently enough to facilitate a fundamental change in your thinking. Films are primarily fictional, and therefore the emotional responses are later rationalized away, especially since they are not supported by evidence, your friends, family or culture. In fact, if you were to continually claim that you felt the presence of a monster in your room, you would be ridiculed, and labeled everything from a scaredy cat to mentally ill!

Many former military personnel, who were continually engaged in combat, on occasion find it difficult to separate themselves from the sights, sounds, and emotions associated with warfare. Obviously they are home safe and sound, but it's just not that easy to dismiss months and sometimes years of exposure to such strong stimuli. How does this equate with religion? Many of us have been taught to believe in something without evidence. To ignore or downplay the bloody history or inconsistencies about our specific religions, and conditioned to believe it's a sin to question the faith. We're told that hell awaits evildoers, and heaven awaits the righteous, even without evidence to support the existence of either realm. On a weekly basis, we're exposed to a congregational theatre having far more perceptual permanence than any movie could ever attain. We subconsciously believe we're doing the right thing, solely because everyone joining us in the pews on Sunday morning believes it too. In the main sanctuary, we unquestionably accept the very pervasive communal energy, and ingest the pastor's doctrinal message. We effortlessly believe every claim of an invasive supernatural presence from the church leaders, because we *feel* it. Or so we think. The more this belief is supported by the culture, the more it directly affects how quickly and total the perceptual change becomes. We slowly believe that this all must be real and learning to never question the conditioning.

This process goes on for years and is reinforced in every facet of your daily life. That's why your belief is so absolute.

When you enter the military, the conditioning is overt. The process of breaking down the old self so a new consciousness can be introduced is not gradual or subtle. Drill sergeants aren't known for their docile demeanors and lovingly patient guidance, and there's a reason for it. They have a few months to turn you from an everyday citizen with your own independent psyche, who has never harmed a fly, into a raging lion capable of following orders without question and taking human lives by the dozens. This is mated to an uncompromising, unshakable sense of camaraderie, where leaving a man behind is not an option—even if retrieving a corpse. Our armed forces don't have the luxury of waiting years to implement their conditioning. This mental programming is often inflamed with rousing speeches and rhetoric before entering combat, with military leaders reiterating why they are in the field, the job they have to do, what's at stake, and who they are fighting for. This exponentially increases a cadet's emotional response and adrenaline while focusing their innate self-preservation mechanism and subconscious training. This directed physiological influence allows them, in a very controlled and incensed state, to perform seemingly superhuman feats of bravery, or push forward when the rest of us might give up.

Let me stop right here, and quickly and unequivocally say, I salute every man and women involved in our military. Their courage and sacrifices are not lost with me, and their heroism affords me the opportunity to exercise this example of free speech. Have you ever watched the science channel measuring the concentration, accuracy, and abilities of our military? It's amazing! Their intense training, conditioning, and mindset are what allow them to be super soldiers.

QUIET SKEPTICS

What do you want from me? Do you really expect me to side with you, the non-believer? Maybe you haven't noticed, but the overwhelming majority of people in this country are believers! Do you really expect me to willingly accept the notion that I, and generations of my family, have been wasting our time, money, and effort involved in a fantasy! What would be the benefits of such a decision? I only see hardship in considering your position. Even if I've had doubts myself, do you realize what you're asking me to do? I'm sorry, a life a being ostracized, socially isolated, or forced to hide my non-belief is just not for me! So I can't for the life of me figure out why you would want me to jump on your un-popular bandwagon. No thanks! I will just continue to go with the flow and not make any waves so I can be accepted by the masses.

I admit this whole religion thing doesn't always make com-plete sense. I'm aware of all the inconsistencies, contradictions, cherry picking, double standards, or special pleading when it comes to my faith. I also quietly recognize my inability to explain or defend the violent or improbable passages, conflicting scrip-tures, or even the validity of the book or the deity as a whole. But I don't care! I look at my faith the same way everyone else does,

accepting the things I like and deem useful, and ignoring the rest.
I need plausible deniability if I'm going to keep the benefits that
come from the placebo effect of believing on faith. I've got too
much invested in this to go against the grain now. The reality is,
if I actually had answers, I would jump at the chance to put you
in your place! But I don't, so I simply condemn Atheists and their
stance, then quickly and conveniently opt out of discussing it in any
more detail. Even if I didn't believe, I would still make the claim
that I was merely spiritual, or believed in a higher power. This
has now become socially acceptable and keeps me from having to
defend the details of Christianity. Since I'm never asked to clarify
or define any particulars about my vague beliefs, I can maintain
societal acceptance while rejecting the specific claims of any one
God or religion. But make no mistake: when pressed, a spiritual
or higher power will always mean that I believe in the God of the
Bible, because it's the only way to be respected or accepted.

   So at the end of the day while you make some good points,
and pose some important questions, I can't acknowledge them to
my circle of friends for fear of being counted among you. So I
publicly must reject you and your position. Because, while fire and
brimstone may not be the true destiny for all Atheists, ridicule, life
upheaval, and social prejudice certainly are!

   One of the trends I've noticed in recent years is this water-
ing down of traditional religious belief and the labels associated
with its practitioners. In decades past, the claim of Christianity
was a revered status, and fostered great pride and respect. Mainly
because it was always associated with the best we believed our
society had to offer. However in recent years it's been repeatedly
associated with unappealing labels like exclusive, hypocritical,
intolerant, ignorant, misogynistic, homophobic, opportunistic,
and many others. These negative traits have come under fire from

other systems of belief, non-believers and even other Christians. This has promoted a growing number of citizens to find a label that identifies their belief in a deity, while distancing themselves from the negative connotations associated with dogmatic man made religions. To that end, society has begun utilizing ever softer labels to denote someone's faith. I'm spiritual, spiritual but not religious, non-religious but not Atheist, anti-theist, a believer in an energy, force, or higher power, I'm a skeptic, freethinker, humanist, and finally Agnostic or Atheist.

This shift seems to be prompted by a ballooning set of factors: the religiously fueled war on terror; the challenge and rise of Atheism; growing abuse claims against religious leaders; laughable or divisive statements made by the fundamentalists or extremists; God's continued absence in the midst of tragedy; poor behavior by many in all faiths, mated to a desire to distance one-self from the divisive rhetoric that attempts to alienate a populace of growing diversity; a selfish need to be allowed to believe any claim or personal belief, no matter how unjustified or prejudicial, without scrutiny or explanation, the younger generation's increasing rejection of the family faith, or the overall rise in consciousness, humanism, and the sense of urgency associated with our precarious global predicament.

A combination of these reasons hav prompted a withdrawing of dogmatism sometimes associated with faith, with many rejecting the improvable notions of their given belief systems, and choosing to focus on the sentiments and practices that seem helpful to the masses. So they have created labels that allowed them to identify with a certain set of beliefs, without alienating or challenging their neighbor.

The unfortunate reality is each label has their own connotations and stereotypes attached to them, which are so often too vague, misused, or misunderstood, that they generally fail to explain anyone's beliefs in their entirety. But maybe that's the point, by claiming some obscure ambiguous label, it allows the individual to personally believe as they see fit.

The religious leaders have also followed suit and have in some cases opted to present the kinder, more inclusive, less belligerent side of belief. So sermons of blasphemy against gays or premarital sex have become simple speeches, filled with mottos and creeds that are good to live by no matter what you believe. This divergence from strict religious scriptures and a lessening of hardcore labels, has assuredly led to many rejecting the notion of a God all together; but would they ever want to publically admit it?

In every church, in every town, members have doubts about their faith. They may have sought guidance or clarity, but never received the answers they were searching for. With shameful looks of disbelief from other church members, they would hastily retract their inquiries about their given faith. Many will immediately stop there, afraid that by moving forward, they might further ostracize themselves from the church community and disrupt their everyday lives in ways that, quite frankly, didn't seem worth it.

Like most Atheists, they were looking for concrete evidence. They were tired of prayers not coming true, being told to just have faith, or being quoted the same scriptures over and over again as viable resolutions to very real issues. Some even get to the point where they no longer believe in their longstanding faith. Nevertheless, they pretend to believe! They go through the motions of church, prayer, etc., because they know a public acknowledgement of any form of non-belief would cause extreme disruption to their lives.

Many standing to the left or right of you during service may not be the stout believers they claim. However, they are terrified of publicly embracing the idea of non-belief! They know all too well what it will mean to make the decision to become agnostic,

Atheist, or to simply reject the claims of Christianity, especially in the ultra-religious African American community. In the back of their minds, they knew their family wasn't simply going to be disappointed, have an argument, and agree to disagree about the topic of religion. This was a common testimony they had heard from other non-believers that were not apart from their strict culture or community. They expected sheer catastrophe, with parents going from absolute shock to unbelievable rage, to even violence in minutes, shoving them around the room and yelling at the top of their lungs as if possessed by some aberrant version of the Holy Spirit. Family members would employ everything from extreme guilt—"Look what you're putting the family through"—to financial blackmail—"Your cut off! You will never get another dime from this family as long as you maintain that foolishness"—to even exorcism—"We're calling Pastor Murphy; he's going to expel that demon that's invaded your soul!"

Once these initial attempts at re-conversion failed, many were completely and utterly isolated, with family member disassociating themselves with them and their apparent new pagan lifestyle. I've personally known several friends that have lost relationships, become homeless, or forced out of schools and organizations after their community discovered their non-belief. Their names are now spoken in back hallways after church services, as the ones that went to the dark side.

Needless to say, such exacting social suicide does not appeal too many. A non-believer at heart might never make his or her feelings public, especially if they have seen for themselves the consequences of those who've tired. Doubters are made to feel almost intolerable shame: for not obeying their parent's wishes and questioning the faith; the continual threat of hell and eternal damnation for not believing in God or his word, and the social and societal isolation from the church family.

For these reasons, many will say to themselves, "What's the harm in believing? It's what's expected, and I don't see any advantage of going against the grain. In fact, all I see is hardship from the ones that have tried."

DIVINE COPING MECHANISM

One of my early concerns, as an Atheist, centered on this idea of hope: are we, as the non-believers, offering viable alternatives to help the faithful cope with life's problems? Religion has been able to provide a perceived supernatural remedy for their woes. What are we offering when we ask them to consider our position?

If someone gains strength from faith, and it motivates them to leave an abusive relationship, overcome a depressive state, or simply get off the couch and exercise their way to a prolonged life, should we remove that catalyst without replacing it with a viable alternative? The placebo effect is well documented, and has proven to be a very useful vehicle for recovery. The mere belief that someone or something is working on your behalf can have a profound and demonstrable affect on the individual, stirring many to unknowingly affect their own outcome, based on perceived help.

How many medical professionals have said, "Medical science has done all it can, the rest of his recovery is up to him, it will solely depend on his will to survive, he has to want to live!" Many theists will claim, "This is when God takes over." And I would agree to a point. If the patient is deeply religious, then a beside prayer from family and friends, coupled with their belief in God, might be all the motivation needed to keep fighting for survival. However, I would argue the same determination to live could be attained through other events: finding out you have a child on the way; a proposal from a longtime love; or winning the lottery. All would offer powerful incentives to stay alive. However, these would simply be conditions they would be fighting for, and not a perceived remedy. Even in certain circumstances where death is unavoidable, belief in a deity could affect the level of fear and anxiety a patient might experience before passing. This is why I'm often quick to support someone's beliefs, if it can make a positive change in their lives. So at the end of the day, is it fair to remove this faith-based coping mechanism without viable alternatives?

While I sometimes struggle with this aspect of faith, I have no reservations about fighting to remove the divisive, "We are better than they are" attitude. Again, if the religious masses would leave others alone, stop knocking on doors and debating their neighbors, observe the separation of church and state, and actively police their own, I think many would be less concerned. Don't get me wrong, there will always be people who won't agree with believing in something without good evidence, but I think the majority would simply say "To each his own," if they were not being affected by someone else's beliefs.

Many theists claim that, deep down, nonbelievers secretly believe in God. When the link between religion and hope is discussed, you'll often hear the adage, "There are no Atheists in foxholes." The saying simply claims that in the midst of the extreme fear or emotion, like the feelings present in warfare, everyone passionately and sincerely calls out to a God, regardless of any prior assertion of non-belief. For argument's sake, let's say this was true, and a proclaimed Atheist called out to God. Is it a genuine affirmation of his true beliefs, or is it the sheer terror and witnessed carnage influencing his plea? Aren't "God darn it" and "oh God" and "Heaven help us" habitual catch phrases that have permeated the media and our social mindset? Does the inmate about to be put to death ask for forgiveness from the attending clergy because of authentic religious convictions and an over-whelming sense of remorse for his victims? Or is it a simple fear of death and the unknown, figuring he might as well jump on the absolution bandwagon to ease his anxiety in the last few minutes of life, covering himself on the off chance that hell exists? Is the confessed guilt of a prisoner without question, even if attained through coercion or relentless torture?

Conversely, should we assume the theist who denounces God in the midst of great suffering was secretly a non-believer all-along? Does the World War II concentration camp prisoner reject his God because he never had faith? Does the devout Christian walking the streets of Afghanistan hide the cross adorning his neck because of wavering faith? Or because the realization that failure to do so might place him in harm's way? Wouldn't God protect a disciple of the one true religion? Wouldn't faith be all he needed? Should this trump card of last resort hold any weight, or represent someone's true beliefs?

Interestingly enough, when theists use the foxhole aphorism, there is never a claim that the Christian soldier has a better chance of survival than the Atheist. Obviously, that sort of declaration could never be substantiated. However, if someone with strong re-ligious conviction survives a vicious front-line conflict, they will instantly make the assertion that it was by the grace of God while dismissing the number of their Christian brothers that lay dead

at their feet. If believers were really blanketed by a divine force,
I can't help but think our military leaders would jump at the
chance to trounce the enemy with these super sanctified soldiers
leading the charge, completely impervious to all weapons formed
against them. But I think we all know the reality is they are just as
vulnerable to roadside bombs as anyone else, even when someone
of a so-called false religion sets the explosive.

Religion is a source of hope and strength for many, and
I certainly understand why emotional support is needed to deal
with these trying times. In all honesty, this was one of the things
I missed about being a part of a religion. Many years ago, logic,
reason, and critical questions were not a part of my evaluation
process. When life changing conditions occurred, it was my internal declaration of faith that gave me a sense of security. I would
simply accept on faith that God would take care of my troubles as
long as I was obedient to his will. This security blanket allowed
me to relieve stress in the face of issues beyond my control. Now
that I require evidence and logical reasons for positive assertions,
I am unwilling to accept feel-good phrases like "Let go and let
God" or "Everything is going to be okay, and it will all work out
in the end."

This has been an advantage, and disadvantage. By removing
the idea that I have an omnipotent benefactor to right my perceived wrongs, has kept me from being complacent about my
circumstances. Forcing me to actively take responsibility for my
actions and work diligently to correct them, because I knew they
would not merely work themselves out on their own. On the other
hand, when I do not have a foreseeable resolution for an issue,
and all hope was lost, I couldn't be easily reassured by politically
correct catch phrases shared to relieve anxiety. If a believer lost

their legs in a car accident, for some, they would gain comfort and hope in the face of this life-changing circumstance, from their faith, even believing that God might intervene and restore their legs through a miracle, while I, as a nonbeliever, would be forced to deal with the emotional stress on my own. What if I grew up in a completely impoverished area, with no real chance of escaping the abuse, drugs, prostitution, and crime that surrounded me on a daily basis, where this environment had become an unfortunate family tendency? While I would continue to search for opportunities to break this generational curse, I would be forced to deal with the mind altering daily stress of my circumstances. Believing that a supreme being will fix my predicament provides me some hope, relieves stress, and allows me to mentally distance myself from the unsettling reality of my situation.

Sometimes, lonely or emotionally battered children make up imaginary friends to help them cope with divorce, being separated from family, or even death. To the child, it represents someone to whom they can talk to, confide in, and be transparent with. It doesn't matter the people are imaginary; the only important thing is the impact this practice makes on the child's psyche. Some therapists might even encourage parents to play along with this belief until the child can come to grips with the traumatic event.

Unfortunately, we don't have that option as responsible adults. If any of us publicly spoke to an invisible friend (other than God), we would instantly receive the gift of a brand new reversible white jacket, with plenty of people insisting we try it on immediately and go for a little ride.

Some believe deities are the product of ancient societies trying to explain their environment, as well as coping with unexplained and frightening phenomena like death, natural disasters, and disease. This may be one of the reasons why so many cultures, no matter how isolated, have created some type of deity. I don't want to downplay the importance of finding ways to affectively deal with stress, and if belief in a deity provides that relief, then I'm all for it.

The problem is that the same comforting system of belief is also divisive and intolerant of other ideologies. If the exclusive, conflict–ridden components could be removed, and religion became a personal introspective pursuit like meditation, it could be fully explored without the need to condemn others for not sharing in a particular system of religious faith.

BLACKS AND RELIGION

I don't understand why a people whose ancestors were brought here against their will, now pray to a God who clearly endorsed these actions through his neutrality? We loudly echo the sentiments of our alleged Christian nation, quickly telling me to go somewhere else if I don't like it! As if I don't have the right to live in a country that owes much of its prosperous infancy to the blood, sweat, tears—not to mention the free labor—of my ancestors.

I don't understand why most cultures worship a God that looks like their people, while we earnestly embrace a God that more closely resembles our ancestral masters then our tribal leaders?

I don't understand, I'm told my ancestors would be ashamed of me! But am I not honoring their refusal to be taken and resistance to captivity? Am I not still fighting the good fight by not accepting the God of their oppressors, and by not reading from a book that was used to justify their servitude? Are you quietly insinuating that the Gods we worshiped in our homeland weren't good enough, since we now embrace the Christian one so unconditionally? Is your obedience to this new master a slap in the face to so many that have sacrificed their lives trying to escape what they were told was a heavenly sanctioned enslavement?

I just don't understand why the institution of slavery wasn't distasteful enough to keep us from rejecting the notion that this

new God was more benevolent than the last, and provides a heav-
enly covering over our people. Clearly his sovereignty endorsed
our captivity by how cavalierly his followers took us as their prop-
erty and so effortlessly denied us our freedom. But I guess we
should be counting our blessings, because without the Europeans
invading our land to save us from our misguided existence, we
would have continued to follow false Gods, which by your own
admission would have assured us a place in hell.

I don't understand, didn't Desmond Tutu once say, "When
the missionaries came to Africa they had the Bible and we had
the land. They said, 'Let us pray.' We closed our eyes. When
we opened them, we had the Bible and they had the land"?
How long will we be seduced by the promise of a better life
continually offered?

I just don't understand, and I probably never will!

As an African American, I'm often told that we owe our freedom entirely to God, and that we are nothing without his grace.
Such testaments are everyday occurrences in my community. I'm
also often asked why African American culture so completely
identifies with Christianity, routinely scoring in the highest per-
centages of surveys that track religious faith, especially since it
was the religion of their oppressors. For us to be such a religious
people, I'm unsure why we are not the most blessed and highly
favored group in God's eyes! When comparing many of the in-
dicators that we might use to track the success of a race, I don't
see divine intervention or heavenly grace listed alongside our percentage of men in jail, percentage of home ownership, level of
education, percentage of single parent homes, overall household
incomes, and so forth. You would think the most religious race
in America (percentage wise) would also be the most inherently
blessed. So what's the reason for such religious devotion in the

face of such obvious inequities? I don't know. All I can do is offer my perspective.

The African continent was invaded, and without regard our people separated from their land and families. While chained like animals on death ships for months at a time, we created new bonds with once tribal foes against a common oppressor. This family of shared horrific circumstance was the new social order that sustained and maintained our humanity and will to live, as we were often starved to death, routinely beaten and thrown overboard. The bones of many a slave litter the ocean floor like breadcrumbs leading away from the only undisturbed home we had known for generations.

As the boats docked in the new land, we were auctioned off as property and forcibly estranged from this new ocean slave community we had come to count on. We were seen as nothing more than another beast-of-burden to be put to work, with far less value than our slave owner's dog. Our families were ripped apart, with members often sold to other plantations. There was no consideration for how devastating and overwhelming this communal separation anxiety would intrinsically change the significance of what the word "Family" would mean in the black psyche. We weren't allowed to read or write, in fact, finding such items in our possession was a crime punishable by everything short of death. After all, the Bible says in Exodus 21:20-21, "And if a man smite his servant, or his maid, with a rod, and he die under his hand; he shall be surely punished. Notwithstanding if he continues a day or two, he shall not be punished: for he is his money." So Biblically, it's fine to beat your slave, even if the injuries incapacitate him for a few days, as long as you don't kill him, because that's a sin worthy of reprimand!

Trying to hold onto the only heritage we knew, we continued our native religious rituals and customs. Much unlike beliefs today, foreign spiritual practices were seen as simple superstitious nonsense to some, and synonymous with satanic worship to others. I'm sure the first Bible and Christian principles were introduced to my ancestors, not out of concern for their immortal souls, but as a last resort to stop them from spiritually contaminating the land with their voodoo-like evil rituals. Or maybe as an ultimate source of hope that would keep them from rising up against their slave owners. I imagine to an utterly conquered people it was slowly accepted, either because our native beliefs were forbidden, or because many emotionally and psychologically conceded to the idea that the God of our masters must be more powerful than our own, since we were chained to a stable wall sharing feed with the livestock. I'm sure this attitude was reinforced by biblical references like Leviticus 25: 44-46 (NLT): "However you may purchase male or female slaves among the foreigners who live among you, you may also purchase the children of such resident foreigners, including those who have been born in your land. Passing them onto your children as a permanent inheritance, you may treat your slaves like this, but the people of Israel, your relatives, must never be treated this way." Or Ephesians 6:5 (NLT): "Slaves obey your earthy masters with deep respect and fear. Serve them sincerely as you would serve Christ."

The slave-owning culture routinely quoted passages from the Bible to support the notion that our servitude was a divine law. Slaves who learned the passages were taught to have no fear because God would reward the faithful in the afterlife. So maybe in some kind of spiritual forfeit, we embraced the thought of pleasing this new lord for eventual reward and to escape further, if not eternal, damnation. I imagine any lingering doubts about the new faith were quickly put to rest by the painful sting of our master's whip.

In any event, we made it our own. Slaves and indentured servants sat together as a new spiritual family, where privileges that separated us during the day were superseded by a sense of kinship and family at night. We were a people of the same hue and heritage, which connected us on a fundamental level. Religion, faith and family shared a cultural symbiosis, becoming the single cemented idea at the core of our forcibly introduced system of belief. To the black community, faith is family! Traditionally, family is the strongest bond we have.

Today, the role of religious overseer is played by our black elders who quickly combat innocently raised concerns about our coveted faith. Any time the younger generation utters their first words of uncertainty, they are quickly and decisively put to rest with a slap across the face and an uncharacteristically aggressive posture. Every subsequent generation learned to adopt this new religious creed without question, as well as to keep their questions to themselves. Christianity has become a pervasive ancestral habit, and considered the purpose defining ideology for our entire race, with many blacks claiming we are literally nothing without God.

Anyway, that's just my perspective of a question best left to scholars and historians, of which I am neither. Even today, the lasting effects of this holocaust can be felt. Recently, I saw a commercial for ancestry.com, where my Caucasian friends can trace their lineage back many generations to a rich heritage, where upon discovery they can locate gravesites and pay spiritual reverence for their dead loved ones. Meanwhile, I can only trace my forefathers back to a slave document, and papers of ownership. In which I have no hope of finding the nameless unmarked graves for the lucky ones, or the places where unlucky blacks decomposed where they were murdered.

While making my spiritual transition, I was surprised to realize that the very thing that was meant to strengthen my faith and conviction was hindering it. The black church was supposed to be my religious sanctuary, guiding me in my walk with the Lord so I could encourage others to honestly seek his covering. It was meant to be the one place where the righteous would lead by example, and where everyone engaged in the never-ending pursuit of community restoration. Yet, I found it very difficult to find a congregation truly working to achieve these noble pursuits.

On the surface, they certainly put their best foot forward. Guests walk into ornately adorned buildings where an eager staff greets you at every turn. Like a newly valued employee showing up for orientation, they are treated like royalty. These public relations specialists enthusiastically sell the church, its spiritual leader, and the pervasive congregational atmosphere.

Unfortunately, like Wall Street, many churches are no different than the capitalistically driven entities, whose shares are publicly traded on the NY Stock exchange. Behind the scenes lies a completely corporate mindset, with backstabbing, lying and social maneuvering used as mandatory tools to get ahead. Money is the name of the game, even when its importance is downplayed as a simple necessity. Many churches that I visited passed the collection plate multiple times during service. Some even required 10% of your monthly paycheck directly deposited into the church's account before allowing membership. Spiritual leaders sought salary increases during periods of economic hardship, despite a significant percentage of their congregation losing their jobs and homes. The church members were continually asked to give in the midst of financial hardship, while their leaders parked their Mercedes in the 4-car garages attached to their million-dollar homes.

Oddly enough, the Bible has this to say on the subject of wealth: "It is easier for a camel to go through the eye of a needle, than for a rich man to enter the kingdom of God." (Mark 10:25) I guess these pastors are more interested in their earthly possessions then their eternal salvation. I never understood why

an omnipotent being needs our money to facilitate the operation
of a house of worship erected in his name?

Then there was the drama. Like a divinely choreographed
soap opera, you waited until next week's service to pick up the
salacious story that left you hanging from the prior week. The
real sermons took place not from the pulpit at the height of service, but in the hallways, offices and parking lots before and after
the pious people of God received their spiritual feeding. If a hug
lasted too long, or an offering was lower than expected, it would
be worthy of gossip. The old adage, "Come as you are," was
replaced by mutterings and criticisms about who was missing
from the pews, the length of someone's skirt, or the tightness of
someone's blouse.

Of course, this attention to fashion was not limited to inap-
propriate attire. Every week, I witnessed a fashion show rivaling
the ones in Paris, France or at the Hollywood award ceremonies,
where this red carpet affair was only missing Joan River's witty
commentary. Hats more elaborate than the last sashayed down the
center aisles of church, for all to see. Men dressed in outrageously
colored suits with matching shoes were regular fixtures, looking
more like pimps than parishioners. However, the most disturbing part of the fiasco was the masquerade of so-called divinely
inspired behavior, where smiles and hellos were quickly replaced
with members cursing at each other, trying to be the first to leave
the parking lot.

It was this hypocritical nature that fed my doubts. I couldn't
understand why someone claiming to be a Christian, who logged
decades in their walk, could struggle so much with niceties I
accepted as a child. I was tired of being the most inexperienced
disciple of Christ, but far more willing to forgive my fellow man,
provide compensation-free assistance, or leave the idea of judgment to my heavenly father.

THE EVERYDAY ATHEIST

Oh…I almost forgot, for a brief second, let's talk about this apparent phenomenon of "Catching the Holy Ghost." In churches across the country, people enter into what seems to be an altered state of consciousness during the height of religious service. They jump around and gyrate to release this divine energy that appears to be coursing through their very soul. For many, including myself at the time, it became another convincing demonstration of God's omnipotent power. When you see Sister Mary cry out, while running up and down the aisles, speaking in tongues as if she's channeling one of the original 12 disciples, it's hard to dismiss the idea that God's presence has unquestionably invaded the sanctuary.

While this communal energy is very real, it's not divine. The parishioners are not overwhelmed by the power of a supernatural being. Rather, they are emotionally influenced by the congregational energy, musical expression, and beautifully expressive oratory from their religious leader, and the real fact that certain churches foster environments where this type of behavior is learned, condoned, and *expected*.

There are many similar examples of group emotional highs in the secular world. During rock concerts, teenagers will run through the gambit of emotions from crying, to uncontrolled joy, to a trance-like peace. Often, they will collapse from sheer exhaustion and need to be carried from the event by security. This is part and parcel of a euphoric musical high, this mob or herd mentality influences people in a particular gathering and environment to behave uncharacteristically. At football games, coaches will huddle their teams together to "psych them up" or stir them into a frenzy, the players will chant, stomp their feet, slap each others' helmets or even head butt during these pre-kickoff pep talks. What about the occasional brawls that occur during overseas soccer matches, where the entire stadium appears to be fighting as the players of their nations settle the score on the field?

During demonstrations, we see a very violent application of this group mindset. How many nightly news clips have you seen depicting a mob of militants burning the American flag in effigy—or a car in real life—while simultaneously chanting and randomly shooting into the air? This is all done without the influence of drugs or divine intervention. It's the energy of an agitated people giving rise to this type of behavior. These behaviors are specific to their environments, so it would be crazy for people to butt heads in church or to see football players falling to the astroturf and speaking in tongues. This is why you rarely if ever see this behavior outside of the context, venues and circumstances where it's considered appropriate, acceptable and expected. When was the last time you walked down the street and saw someone catch the Holy Sprit? Not convinced, then why, if this power were so overwhelming, aren't other religions and denominations susceptible to these incensed states? When was the last time you saw the Pope catch the Holy Ghost? Are you more in touch with God than he is?

Like many things in our society, this particular phenomenon is specific to particular religious cultures, and draws from the same emotional reservoir as faith healing and exorcism. The communal frenzied energy, coupled with the placebo effect, generates artificial results. If you don't believe me, ask your pastor to meet you at the local hospital so he can heal a couple floors of patients. If the power is truly divine, and he or she has the gift, it won't matter if the sick and dying have faith. The undeniable reality is that the majority of Christian denominations think that catching the Holy Ghost, speaking in tongues and exorcism, are completely phony! So it's not just the Atheists standing in disbelief.

Why do we feel we can't perform on our own? Unfortunately, religious belief has been used to control the poorer end on the general public. When you give people a God that they believe is looking out for them in all circumstances, will fix their current situations no matter how desperate, forgive them of any transgressions, and reward their unwavering obedience and faith in the afterlife, chances are you will have a people that will not rise up and demand change on the manmade hardships in their lives. Why is it important, because we have some very real issues in our community! We need better education, housing, jobs, and health care, not more prayer. We have been praying for hundreds of years, and our communities need tangible help. So let's try something new.

I'm often asked, "If you could snap your fingers tomorrow and put and end to religion, would you?" My answer is a resounding "No." Believers claim that without God, they are nothing. He is the sole provider of their strength, lifelong accomplishments, and continued hope; that only his involvement can provide any legitimacy and purpose to their existence; and without his commandments outlining their morality, there would be nothing suppressing and controlling their behavior.

While some of us don't need to believe in a supreme being to add purpose to our lives, guide our behavior, or draw daily strength from, there are others that do. I don't think it's fair to remove this sense of security, especially when I don't think we would necessarily like the results. The problem is in addressing the divisive nature of religion, and stopping the legislation of faith-based laws.

I never started this book to bring down religion, but rather to tell my personal story. I simply want to be accepted like everyone else, for who I am, not just condemned as an Atheist. I think religion should be a private introspective pursuit, and not a money driven, man-made construct with strong political ties. Would I put an end to church? Of course not! They are an existing infrastructure, seen as crucial to the lives of many. It would be foolhardy not to use their advantage.

With a little effort, churches could become the largest vehicles for change in our dilapidated communities. They could develop into cultural centers, where we could speak about the accomplishments and mental strength of our ancestors. The older generation could continue to have fellowship, but the focus would not be centered on an invisible God who is given credit for all man's accomplishments, but around them, as the revered forefathers and civil right leaders for the freedoms we now enjoy. These new secular community centers would begin to systematically address the concerns that plague our neighborhoods. I envision doctors, lawyers, and family counselors working in former places of worship, donating much of their time to help their community. We could sing lost Negro spirituals, and new songs written about our promising future. We could praise tangible leaders like Martin Luther King. Churches could become an intricate network of support for the entire community, with each having a specific role in the health and welfare of the people. Our entire community would immerse and inundate our youth with social and behavioral education, changing their very mindset, so the next generation could achieve. "Keeping our eyes on the prize and staying resolute in the pursuit," as Dr. King said.

We would meet our cultural goals. Guest speakers would be leaders from our homeland, and offerings would be used to operate the facility, send school organizations to national events, and revitalize our streets. If a megachurch (with careful planning) could take the prior week's offerings and accumulated building and landscaping supplies, and descend on a city block one weekend out of the month, how long would it take before the entire face of our community was changed? Imagine how nice it would be if the rundown, drug infested park became green again and safe for our children. While this might seem like a tough transition, we made it through centuries of slavery, so I have no doubt we can do this.

Many might think I'm fostering and or promoting racial division. I'm not. We are still a part of an amazing race—the human one. The sci-fi nerd in me revels in the hope that one day *Star Trek* science fiction will become a scientific fact. We would travel the stars and do away with the petty social squabbles that continue to divide us. We could then explain our historical mistakes to other intelligent life forms throughout the cosmos. Human kind would or could become the benchmark by which all sentient life is judged.

MORALITY

Ah...Morality. This is often paraded as a fundamental benefit of religion. With many theists asking the loaded question: Without belief in God, where would society or individuals get the foundation for their behavior? It amazes me the number of times I have heard someone say, "If you're right, and there is no God, then why should we be kind to each other?" or "If we evolved from animals and not the product of a loving God, why aren't we acting like animals?" Funny enough, when I was a young Atheist, the question that gave me pause was, "So you're telling me your civil behavior is only because you believe a God exists, or from your fear of him?"

I actually thought that if the theistic masses strongly believed this view, they would suddenly be capable of any deplorable act if they began to doubt the existence of their God. Would the believer, in the midst of uncertainty, behave badly to prove a point, or because there were no longer any perceived heavenly consequences? A sort of self-fulfilling prophecy, if you will! For the most part, I rejected this idea, hoping that the very real earthly laws and law enforcement would be enough to deter someone from acting foolishly.

I'm so confused and on the fence by this discussion surrounding morality. When I began to tackle this subject, I was surprised at how complex it was. I never really gave it much thought until now. I was simply taught not to cause anyone harm, to treat people the way I would want to be treated, etc. I was not prepared for how convoluted this research would be. As I examined my first book, article, or website, I was instantly thrown to the epistemological wolves! Concepts like objective and subjective morality, moral relativism, moral naturalism, moral absolution, ethical consciousness, moral lawgiver, evolutionary ethics, consequentialism, Cultural/Ethical/Individual relativism, neurology, error theorists, rationalism, moral landscape, and others, were thrown in my face at a dizzying pace. While many concepts are synonymous with one another, they sufficiently muddy the waters of this often-academic debate.

When I spoke to my friends, most claimed our morals came from religious faith, or were simply the product of our environment or culture, and this was what I was looking for. I wanted to know what the everyday person thought about this subject, not the convoluted ideas tossed around at the highest intellectual levels. While I, of course, wanted the true facts about the subject, I more importantly wanted to know how it related to most people. My interest centered on how this discussion could be useful to the masses, so real progress could be made.

One of the key issues I instantly noticed when tackling this convoluted subject was the misuse of terms. I have continuously seen distinct confusion over the subtle differences between morality and ethics. While they are so regularly used interchangeably at the highest level of discourse on the subject, the reality is they are different, and those differences seem to play a substantial role in this conversation. I would like to take a moment to discuss these terms as I have come to understand them. However the scope of this topic is utterly enormous and cannot be addressed in this work. Instead, I want to simply attempt to set some groundwork for our discussion, so I may better explain why I don't believe objective morality comes from God, and that with some clarity in our wording, it might help lead to an ethical construct that could guide humanity to a prosperous future society.

Morality is more simply the system of labeling good or bad conduct. Morality needs no qualifiers or justification; it's merely what we personally judge to be right or wrong. It appears to be most often a product of society, upbringing, religious beliefs, etc. Anyone could make a moral argument for just about anything, due to its largely subjective nature, because it is simply based on someone's personal perception of what constitutes good or bad behavior.

Ethics are the guidelines by which we determine the validity of a moral label. Ethics are the justification arm of the morality mechanism. Ethical constructs are the method we use to determine and support a moral choice, as well as the system used to filter new experiences through, to determine their morality, and hopefully help shape the world we want to live in now, and in the future. Without getting too technical, ethical philosophies or the thought processes surrounding how ethical models are derived, are somewhat varied, but all based on some demonstrable reason. They consist of things like determining the greatest amount of joy while diminishing harm, or how righteous or altruistic an action might be. Others are focused on the consequences of an action to determine its ethical stance. Some ethical ideas maintain that cultures dictate ethics and in turn morality. However the majority of the ethical constructs seem to be focused on logically protecting the well-being of humans as the primary conduit to an ethical philosophy, and a working model to determine morality.

The problem that I see when examining this argument is someone opens up the conversation by saying something like:

"Morality is completely subjective, and who are we to make
the determination that someone else's actions are immoral."

But, of course, they are referencing the literal definition of
morality as simply labels placed on conduct.

But the opposition takes a heart-wrenching example and says,

"No you're mistaken, there are certainly objective moral
truths, like slavery is obviously wrong and not subjective,"

Going on to say its institution denies the freedoms of a group
of individuals without reasonable cause. But what they really mean
is that the practice is unethical, because it stands in opposition of
human well-being, and should not be preformed or condoned by
rational thinking people. Obviously this is a very simplistic example, but the point I'm trying to make is that both parties are
correct. Without qualifiers, slavery can be considered subjectively
moral or immoral, based on someone's personal perspective, culture, or time period, but the act has always been unethical when
pressed against most of the philosophies used to determine ethics.
However, I understand the importance and desire of many to definitively prove objective moral constants (even when they mean
ethical constants), which are shared by all humanity., primarily
due to the useless ability of morality, the simple activity of labeling conduct, to facilitate any significant positive changes. By
stating that morals are subjective, and that no matter how foreign
a practice is to us, it can be considered moral in whatever environment deems it so, can bottleneck the conversation. Subjective
morality simply regulates any opposing view as differing, but as
a very equal opinion. However, some see this as an attempt to
close the door on opposing an act that is harmful and contradicts
human well-being. Because for many, morals and ethics are in-
tertwined, and as rational people, why should we be concerned

with the labels, and not the justification for why we would impose each label. By establishing an ethical construct for morality focused on well-being, steeped in logic, while carefully factoring in the consequences of an action, pressed against the goal of the desired future society, as rational, thinking, sentient beings, I imagine we could make real progress. For the ease of conversation, I will continue my argument without referencing morality or ethics individually.

Every moral argument for the existence of God seemed to just assume there were objective moral values that could have only come from him. Unfortunately, I could never really get anyone to elaborate on the subject. They only made large, broad-based claims, such as, "Everyone knows cruelty is wrong," ignoring the fact that we all don't consider the same things cruel. This was the problem I faced in understanding the concepts of morality or ethics in general, even when devoid of religious overtones. My principal issue was determining the line between subjective or objective morality, the idea that what's considered moral or ethical changes between differing people, beliefs, cultures, or societies, against the idea that there are certain universal moral truths present in all humanity. On a grand scale, objective morality made sense to me: the random killing of a stranger walking down the street is wrong, ignoring the infinitesimally small minority of the population that would disagree on purely self-indulgent masochistic reasons, or that the majority of the planet can agree that rape and slavery are wrong, but what about moral ideas that are not as clearly defined?

Can we still claim objective moral certainty? As the number of people that disagree with a particular moral idea increases, when does it become a subjective principle? If .001%, 2% 10%, or 25% of our population disagree on a particular moral claim, at what point does it become subjective? Yes, there are exceptions to any moral idea, but what is the moment of critical mass when the exception becomes a recognized observable alternative?

Another frustration I had during my reading was how many times semantic arguments were used to try and prove a point. Many authors offered the rarest anomalies to refute any example of objective morality, while many seemed to think that right and wrong were largely viewed as subjective concepts that can vary greatly from culture to culture, I didn't understand the emphasis on the extreme outer edges of this dialogue. If someone suggests killing is wrong, the urge to play Devil's advocate seems to be a standard practice. Suddenly, it means we can't take someone's life if they are threatening to blow up a school bus full of children? We shouldn't steal, so if you take someone's car keys without asking, because they know they're too drunk to drive, you're morally bankrupt. We shouldn't lie, but can the hostage nego-tiator lie or make promises they have no intention of keeping in order to save lives?

In daily conversation, I understand what the overwhelming majority of people are talking about when they make the previ-ously mentioned assertions. We can always scrutinize something to the point of inoperable stagnancy, halting any potential progress that could have been made on a given subject. Politicians do it everyday, and you see how little they accomplish. If we are go-ing to move forward, we need to devise a way of discussing this subject while focusing on the key issues, and maybe only address-ing the rare anomalies on a case-by-case basis.

Back to the subject at hand: Does our morality come from God? I really didn't (and I guess still don't) understand this argument. The theists I spoke to seemed to believe in the idea that the divine has bestowed a moral law upon all mankind. It was hammered into our souls by our heavenly blacksmith, and is intrinsically present in all humanity. It alone allows us to differentiate between right and wrong, good and evil. Believers claim that without this moral law, everything would be a matter of opinion and therefore, permissible.

However, I could never figure out how this divine objective morality worked. How does God get this information to his followers? Is it unchanging, or does it vary depending on the time period? Is this moral law just for the chosen people, or all humanity? Is the very existence of morality itself supposed to be evidence of God? Quite frankly, I wasn't sure how anyone could justify that their God was the only path to ethically sound societies, or that without belief in a deity it would ultimately lead to depravity and social unrest?

Surely, this experiment has been run multiple times by the vastly differing faiths and ideologies that have given rise to civil and prosperous societies. Or by the tens of thousands of years humanity survived and thrived without the presence of our modern-day deities or belief systems. Or maybe by the growing numbers of people who have chosen to leave religious faith entirely. Maybe I just missed the host of headlines that read, "Another Atheist kills on their inaugural day of non-belief." So I'm still looking for the evidence supporting this argument.

When a believer claims that God morally guides them, I assume they must be referring to what they believe is taught through their religious doctrine: their God's example through his actions, or what they believe to be the implied true nature of their God. If not, and the moral authority can be attributed to something outside of the faith, they would no longer be able to make the assertion that only belief in God can create and sustain morality. Early in my investigation, I noticed that countries like Sweden, Denmark and Norway were predominantly Atheistic, and yet they had healthy, morally sound, civilized societies, often surpassing the United States in markers like per capita, life expectancy, academic proficiency, low crime rates, etc. This of course stands in direct opposition of the original assertion about morality.

Nevertheless, I began to explore these ideas separately, first examining the Bible and the God portrayed within its pages. On many occasions, God has ordered or permitted the killing of men, women and children. He encouraged slavery. He held children responsible for the misdeeds of their parents. At times, he was controlling, unforgiving and intolerant of different religions, sexual orientations, and races. Frequently, he dispensed horrible plaques to the guilty and innocent alike. He often shared in our most objectionable human emotions such as jealousy, vengeance, bigotry and anger. But supposedly he's the physical embodiment of love and the guiding moral compass for all of Christianity?

If this is the source of our morality, I'm surprised our civilization has lasted this long. The truth is the Bible doesn't guide your morality. The scriptural passages and stories that depict the atrocities mentioned above are either ignored, considered outdated or manipulated during church service to emphasize a more wholesome message. For example, the biblical story of Job, which was continually offered to me as one of the greatest examples of faith under trail, meant to illustrate how God rewards the faithful, and while we might go through tests at times, our heavenly father is always there to protect us.

Now let's examine this story more closely. Job was the most righteous man on earth. He feared God without question and passionately followed his will. He was also considered one of the most blessed and wealthy in all the land. He had a loving wife, large family, and an abundance of cattle, sheep and camels. One day, while God and Satan were talking, God said to Satan, "Have you considered my servant Job, that there is none like him in the earth, a blameless and an upright man, one that fears God, and turns away from evil?"

The Devil agrees, but maintains that the only reason he's so faithful is because he had been so lavishly blessed. He went on to say that if God took all of his blessings away, he would surely curse him. So God decides to permit Satan to test Job, allowing him to remove anything from his life he liked, as long as he didn't lay a finger on Job.

Overnight, Job lost everything. All his children were killed in a collapsing home, his servants were murdered, his livestock stolen, and his wife left him. Still, Job praised God. "The Lord giveth and the Lord taketh away" was his attitude, assuming that he must have committed some wrongdoing to be punished so harshly. After failing in his first attempt to convince Job to denounce his heavenly father, Satan returned to God, and through an identical conversation was given permission to inflict harm on Job's body as long as he didn't kill him.

For the second test, Satan inflicted Job with horribly painful boils over his entire body. At this point, Job's friends were so distraught, that they wept over his predicament. It was at this time Job questioned why God was punishing him. God instantly appeared before Job and ridiculed him for questioning his will, and rants about his power: "Who is this that questions my wisdom with such ignorant words?" (Job 38:2, NLT) "Where does light come from, and where does darkness go?" (Job 38:19, NLT) "Are you as strong as God? Can you thunder with a voice like his?" (Job 40:9, NLT).

Job apologized for questioning God, and then was blessed by God with four times as much as he had before.

My problem with this trite tale centers on why God felt the need to impress an evil nemesis, which once tried to overthrow his kingdom at the expense of his most righteous follower, Job. I thought God couldn't stand to be in the presence of sin or evil; yet, he had more than one encounter with Satan in which he made a malevolent wager on Jobs' life. Why did Job fear God? Why should we be impressed with someone who vehemently obeys the more powerful and vengefully oppressor? Why would God allow Satan to test his most faithful servant a second time when Job had successfully passed the first test? When Job finally reached a breaking point, and simply asked why he was being tortured, God mocked him for not being as powerful as he is, and then shamed him into an apologetic stance. Once God was satisfied, Job was blessed with wealth and another family.

I wonder how many people would be okay if God had tested them in such a manner. Would it be okay for him to kill your children so he could make a point to an evil force? God never resurrected Job's original children that he allowed Satan to murder. Yet, when this story was referenced during church services, the unflattering parts about God's character were conveniently omitted or never questioned.

What about the story of Abraham, in which God supposedly needed to test his faith by ordering him to take his son Isaac to the land of Moriah and sacrifice him as a burnt offering? Once Abraham arrived in Moriah, God stopped him at the last moment and said; "Now I know you love God."

Is it just me, or does this sound a little crazy? If I were a believer, and an entity claiming to be my God ordered me to murder my own son, I would have laughed in his face and said, "You may not have known this, but my God is all-knowing and would never need to test the will of any of his followers. He is also the embodiment of goodness and love, and would never ask me to surrender my child's life as a testament of my faith. So go try and fool someone else, Satan!"

How about the story of Lot's escape from Sodom and Gomorra. Church leaders conveniently skim over the fact that Lot offered his virgin daughter to the crazed male mob so they would not try to intimately know the two angels that had come to warn Lot's family of the impending destruction. Surely, God would be able to protect angels sent to do his bidding. As the family escaped the city, Lot's wife was turned into a pillar of salt for committing the unthinkable sin of glancing over her shoulder to witness the utter destruction of the place she had called home. I know God asked her not to look back, but does this punishment really fit the crime? After their successful escape, Lot fell into a drunken stupor and ends up having sex with, and impregnating both his daughters on two separate nights! If this was the most righteous man of God that he sought to save, then I'm further confused about the origin of divine morality.

Of course the answer I here most often when believers try to justify God's questionable actions is, "God created us and everything in the Universe. Because we are his creation, and he has sovereignty over all mankind, the normal rules of human morality don't apply to him!"

If this is the case, how could you ever make a determination about the demeanor of God, good or bad? Because we only have human morality to use as the yardstick, which of course the believer says doesn't apply to him. The aforementioned statement appears to simply be making a poor excuse for God, allowing the theist to avoid answering for God's actions. Of course your thinking why would God have to answer for his behavior. Because he demands our obedience, worship, servitude and conversion, and will ultimately send us to hell for non-compliance? Would you follow a leader who never explained his actions, even when they seemed cruel and unjust? If so, you're the perfect candidate to join a doomsday cult or fall under the influence of an evil dictator. Not to mention that once you claim God lives by a completely different moral code than ours, I don't understand how He can still be used as the ethical yardstick or model for human morality?

I've never understood how theists can claim the Bible is the objective, rock-solid source of their morality, while at the same time ignoring the ease at which they cherry pick their holy doctrine. They quickly dismiss the unpalatable biblical teachings and questionable behavior. The very conscious decision and ability to differentiate appalling acts in the Bible as no longer viable or wrong, in direct opposition of its teachings and the claim that its word is unchanging and forever pertinent, is proof of their innately secular morality. I don't understand why they don't see that this behavior is an illustration that their ethics are derived from humanity and not divinity. Not to mention when you blatantly excuse or ignore the violence and atrocities committed by your God with no explanation, how are you suddenly qualified to be the moral standard by which everyone else should be judged?

The next claim, that the true nature of God is love and kindness, ignores one obvious question: How do you know God's true nature is one of benevolence if it's not revealed in his actions or his holy text? I can only assume that this determination is made through one's personal experiences with God. "I know God is good because he saved my grandfather from cancer, or helped me through hard times," says many.

Unfortunately, these are simply deeds being attributed to God. They happen to everyone, regardless of religious affiliation. Again, God gets all the credit and none of the blame. I could just as easily remove the word "God" and replaced it with anything that I thought would be capable of facilitating such a change. Vishnu, Zeus, or my dead ancestor had a hand in my recovery; even aliens intervened in my life would all fit the bill. Without any proof that what I'm claiming is true, why should it be accepted? I believe Christopher Hitchens once wrote, "That which is presented without evidence can also be rejected without evidence."

Many famous Atheists like Sam Harris continually point out that the animal kingdom has their own instinctual moral system that governs their society, allowing them to survive and thrive. They have comparable disapproval for things like adultery, theft, and assault. When animals are starving, most never turn to each other for a quick meal. This instinctual moral character, which allows them to discern between right and wrong and aid the well being of their species as a whole, appears to be very present in most life.

I would also argue, who is intrinsically the better human being? The individual who believes an omnipotent being with a history of vengeance is listening to their very thoughts, forcing them to observe a synthetic moral code because they fear eternal hell and damnation, and crave admittance into an afterlife utopia? Or the person who has decided to be a kind, generous and constructive member of society because it allows their civilization to flourish? I would also be more inclined to believe the theist claim of superior God given morality, if they outperformed secular individuals of similar educational, economic, psychological, geographic and cultural backgrounds in matters of morality. If theists were better neighbors, had longer marriages with significantly lower divorce rates, and better behaved, more accomplished children, I would be more willing to entertain their claim of ethical superiority.

What about the men in history characterized as evil, like Hitler? He was supposedly an Atheist who ordered the death of millions. First of all, he was not an Atheist. If you read the transcripts of his speeches, he claims to be a Roman Catholic who saw his war on the Jews as "doing God's work." But for arguments sake, let's say someone like Hitler was a non-believer and went on a killing spree. Do we simply assume his Atheism is the cause? I don't see how you can just pluck someone out of history and say, "Look, he did bad things to good people and he was an

Atheist, so there must be something wrong with Atheism." Hitler also wore a mustache. Is everyone with the same facial hair a potential genocidal megalomaniac?

For me, it boils down to the validity of their claims. Are they right or wrong? Can they justify their position with evidence or not? I think we can all agree that there are crazy people on both sides of this argument, and I certainly don't blame Catholicism for the act of one crazed Austrian who tried to take over the world during the first half of the 20th century. Nor am I ignoring the positive acts done by people of all faiths. I'm simply pointing out that all of the good done by theism–helping the homeless, feeding the hungry, revitalizing neighborhoods–can be attained without the divisive constructs of organized religion or belief in God. We already have societies that show it works, and works well!

Morality is defined as: "the concern with or the distinction between good and evil or right and wrong; right or good conduct." Arguably the favorable byproduct, and dare I speculate the eventual goal of ultimate morality (if there could be such a thing) would be the attainment of lasting peace. Think about it: what would we have if everyone were solely concerned with being moral (in its absolute broadest sense), only performing acts that served the best interest of our species, by only supporting ideas that led to human, animal and environmental well-being, aggressively avoiding anything that would be harmful in any capacity to another person, sharing resources of all kinds and effortlessly helping strangers? We would have peace. I will even take it a step further and ask you to consider an ever-increasing condition of peace. The idea of everyone living harmoniously with Nature and each other across the entire planet with the singular mindset of bettering all mankind and their surroundings, could result in a utopia, paradise, or a perfect kingdom.

So it may be in the best interests of all of us to nail down this concept of good and bad, right or wrong, moral or immoral. Conversely, immorality at its highest levels, in which everyone is concerned with inflicting as much pain and anguish on as many people as possible, quickly translates to war, and hell on earth!

In my opinion, the biggest determent to the first goal is the number of people that blindly follow religious belief. While it has certainly played a major role in shaping our modern day morality, my question is, should it have been allowed? Because unfortunately some of the most oppressive and immoral acts in our history have been intensified and sustained by religious faith. Too often, scripture has been used to justify things like slavery, misogyny, murder, and wars. Unchecked, these prejudices swell into history's all-too-familiar religiously fueled atrocities: the Jewish holocaust, Crusades, Inquisitions, Salem Witch Trials, African slave trade, and the countless conflicts in the Middle East and in Africa.

Many will say that this is simply a demonstration of religious faith gone amuck, misused or poorly interpreted. But isn't this the fundamental danger inherent with believing something on faith? If it's just something you're supposed to feel, or arbitrarily pull from religious texts, how can you claim someone else's emotions or interpretations are more or less valid than your own? Just because you personally believe God doesn't condone these social ills doesn't mean you're right. In fact, you would be required to defend this notion, since your religious opposition would have scriptural references on their side and examples from God's own memoirs. The major leaps in morality, like abolishment of slavery or equal rights for women, were made *in spite of* prevailing religious belief, not because of it!

When discussing morality, I find that religious belief so often ends the conversation before it begins. There is not a single religion in which all of its members are in complete agreement about all the expectations and laws of their governing deity. It cannot even be agreed that everyone is born (not created) equal and deserves the same privileges and rights. Or that women deserve equality in every facet of our society. Why? Because, for many, religious belief supersedes everything, and the overwhelming majority of the earth's population is too close to this global hot button. Just as companies have a fiscal obligation to their investors to make them money, even if in direct opposition to the best interests of our country's economy, churches see a spiritual obligation to their God to cultivate as many new disciples as possible, even if directly conflicting with the best interests or well-being of our species!

This is why moral uniformity based on religious faith would be a useless pursuit. No one is willing to budge or compromise on what they believe are the teaching of their deity.

A believer might ask, "Why do we need to change things now? Our system of religious morality and faith has served us well for centuries."

What does that mean? How do you determine if a system has served your society well? Am I to assume that solely because your community is still intact and has not rendered itself extinct (yet), that it must be working well? If other societies that don't share your particular system of religious morality surpass you in every measurable indicator, can we assume you got it wrong, or there might be a better way? If I were to interview the most oppressed class or group in your culture, would they give your society such a glowing report card? Do the women stripped of rights and privileges, the starving underclass, largely discriminated against ethnicities, sexually ostracized or religiously oppressed minorities, share your "If it ain't broke, don't fix it" attitude?

Ask yourself: do you believe your religion is the way the truth and the light, and that none will hold eternal life and enter the kingdom of God but through Christ Jesus? If so, do you believe your religious counterparts share this same unwavering faith based on their own holy principles? If so, are you willing to compromise on any part of your belief system to include others who share a different faith? If not, how would those conflicting ideologies continue to aggressively grow and coexist peacefully, especially when you inherently believe they must be wrong, because you must be right?

As our planetary numbers increase along with our global aspirations, so does the need for more uniform principles or behavior. If theists believe they hold the divinely inspired moral high ground, and are unwilling to compromise on their faith-based ideology, then they must answer a question: how can opposing inflexible religions be compatible with peace in the midst of an exponentially growing and mixing populace? I will be the first to say that religion is just one of the major issues facing our global community that we must address if we are to pull ourselves off the road to extinction! I personally think financial greed and the needless pursuit of power are the front-runners in self-destructive behavior. Unfortunately, religion and faith are often used to mask, repress, aggravate and misdirect the real issues plaguing many of our planetary communities. But it's very important to be able to identify the people that are not on board with our goal of species sustainability.

One thing I have always found trouble accepting is the notion that everyone is born sinful. When we are faced with amazing adversity or challenges, and have the ability to help, we tend to pull together the most. During 9/11, I heard about amazing acts of bravery and self-sacrifice. It didn't seem like our inherently sinful, evil nature was taking hold. People were helping strangers! Others just wanted to show their support in any way they could, even applauding the fire trucks as they sped to ground zero. At the time,

I worked for an industrial supply company, and all of our locations were struggling to keep one item on the shelves—the American flag! It didn't matter how small or big they were; everyone had to have one. Maybe my judgment is being clouded by emotions of patriotism and the human tragedy of those events, but I didn't see the inherently sinful, self-centered nature of our species at work. As I've said before, I believe in us, and not in a God in the sky.

9/11: THE GAME CHANGER

On September 11th 2001, our nation was attacked. Beside the fact that it was the worst terrorist attack in United States history, it seemed to be a turning point for the country. It was this violent mechanism that for many started the 21st century rise in faith and the faithless.

For one of the first times in our history, the impenetrable armor of the United States border was circumvented and the fight brought to us. We have been comfortably sipping our Chai Lattes and driving our BMWs, oblivious to the world outside our borders, too often detached from the realities and hardships that have become commonplace for so many. We were all too happy to remain in our suburban ignorance.

The attack changed all of that. For the first time, Americans felt real fear, fear that many in this country had never been exposed to, except for the dwindling number of citizens that witnessed the attack at Pearl Harbor in 1941. September 11th showed us a glimpse of what some areas of the world experience on a daily basis. The sheer horror of these events overwhelmed many Americans, and quite frankly it shook me, too. You instantly wonder is this it? Was this the end of civilization? Were the nukes about to drop? Was the proverbial "End Time" really here? Is life as we know it over?

I was in Atlanta when the attacks occurred, far removed from the actual horror of what really went on. While every news channel relentlessly covered the tragedy, it couldn't have compared to what the real scenes must have been like on the streets of New York City. From my living room, I saw people sitting on sidewalks with a little blood on their business suits, covered in dust, and limbs wrapped in bandages. Most of the footage consisted of people walking over bridges en masse, emergency services racing to the scene and, of course, the countless times they replayed the planes crashing into the buildings or the cascading destruction of each tower. But I always wondered what it must have been like to have really been there, and witness the uncensored scenes. CNN couldn't show you the severed limbs that littered the sidewalks, or the severely mutilated, horrible burned individuals that staggered from ground zero looking for help. What about the images of the crumpled bodies that stained the sidewalk where many jumped to their deaths as a way of escaping the torture of being burned alive? Or the determination it must have taken for the first responders to sift through tons of rubble and check every disfigured body for any signs of life. I continually stand in awe at the heroism of the men and women in our emergency services. They are certainly made of some sterner stuff!

9/11 was the game changer. Up until then, religion was mostly a quiet personal pursuit that few really talked about. While our country enjoyed great diversity with many varied beliefs, we coexisted relatively peacefully with a "You do your thing, and I'll do mine" attitude. Atheism and agnosticism were only openly practiced by a fringe segment of our population. Extremist behavior and attitudes, at least in the country, were not as common. So many of us never felt we had the right or even the need to question our neighbor's beliefs. We proudly clung to the constitutional notion that in America, every citizen should be allowed freedom of religion.

All of that changed after the attack. Everyone seemed to know someone affected by the tragedy. It was no longer a *Nightline* documentary profiling the ongoing atrocities in some war-torn country thousands of miles away. It was right here in our backyard, and very, very personal! 9/11 propelled the United States into war! For many Americans we were no longer fighting a specific location in the Middle East, or a militant terrorist organization, but an entire ideology. Right or wrong, the perception for some was we were not simply fighting Al-Qaeda, but Islam itself, because it was the spiritual foundation of the 9/11 terrorists.

Suddenly, everything from the Islamic world became newsworthy. Before the attacks, many Americans didn't really care about what happened in this obscure place we called the Middle East, as long as their rich oil deposits kept flowing our way. But now, knowing our "enemy" was priority #1. Only days after the attacks, Muslim Americans were subject to hate crimes all across the country, they became the newfound targets of a nation's indiscriminate anger over the amazing loss of life at ground zero. Overnight, anyone of Muslim descent was deemed to be somehow responsible for the attacks, and was chosen to atone for the terrorist's crimes. Americans were looking for revenge and some payback, so it was not surprising that we were thrust into another war shortly after the attacks. This further fueled the sometimes bias reporting that supported the war in Iraq. Stories that only a year earlier would have been buried on page 6 in your local newspaper became headline news. Articles and interviews outlining the subjugation of women, be-heading of prisoners, Al-Qaeda training camps, and anti-American demonstrations were commonplace. We all saw the late night news footage depicting a crowd of militants with weapons, chanting "Death to the United States!" while burning the American flag in effigy.

Suddenly debates about Islam, and religion in general, bombarded the airways. The once untouchable subject of faith was being debated in halls across the country. People were glued to their TV sets to watch documentaries about the harshly repressive society of Afghanistan, further fueling the hatred in so many that were touched by the events of 9/11. Before the attacks, someone proposing an Islamic place of worship anywhere in the country would have faced little concern. Now, more than a decade after 9/11, the topic still draws front-page news and is a hotly contested land development, even hundreds of miles from ground zero.

The events of September 11th forced many of us from our suburban neutrality. The fear that it could happen again was the catalyst that coerced many to take a very hard and conscious look at religion, belief, and its realities. Does freedom of religion have real consequences? Can we, or should we continue to allow religious freedom to all? What does my system of belief stand for? Have I done enough to push my lifesaving faith on the lost masses? Can I continue to hide my non-belief? Can I continue to claim impartial ignorance about this issue of faith? The event turned the dial up on the dormant emotions and questions that, quite frankly, never needed definitive answers before now. Many around me seemed to amplify what they were already feeling.

Some of my devout Christian friends became religious fundamentalists. More convinced than ever that the spread of their religious doctrine would be the only way to halt the ever-advancing evil system of belief that led to the attacks. They were far less concerned with allowing everyone equal religious representation, or freedom. More than ever, someone's faith became his or her moral resume, completely overshadowing who they were or how they acted.

Agnostics were jolted from what is often perceived as a spiritual straddling of the fence. 9/11 made it more difficult for the already religiously complacent to stay neutral on this issue of faith. Some chose to distance themselves from religion, with many questioning their religious leaders' bigotry and denouncement of the attacks as a result of evil people. They were ashamed at the ease with which these church leaders calmly ignored the bloody history that had made Christianity what it is today. With a "wiping their hands of it" attitude, they broke their ties to dogmatism and superstition, and moved to some form of non-belief. Once quiet Atheists felt like the time had come to create a real voice for themselves. They came out of the proverbial closet and took a stand for logic and reason, going on the offensive to discuss why religion was a Bronze Age ideology that needed to die with that time period.

Still others decided to take a good hard look at the event. They were willing to not only ask, but logically evaluate the one question that the faithful often ignored while praising and blessing the relief efforts after a tragedy: If God truly exists, why would he have allowed it to happen in the first place? Especially when it would mean so many things to so many people? The militants that carried out the attack (and some societies throughout the world) applauded the event, claiming it was the will of Allah, while the majority of people in the US had a very different take. Some Christians said the attack was a push for Americans to take action against evil, or that God knew there would be a surge in religious belief, or it was punishment for our materialistic ways and turning away from him. The list goes on and on.

But which side is right? The reality is these are just emotional faith-based claims without a shred of evidence to support them. You can't simply claim there is a God out there, who is for or against the attacks on September 11th, because it makes you feel good. This is propaganda often fed to the masses by politicians looking for re-election. Why is this an issue? Because, unfortunately, many people started to believe these unfounded claims and they allowed such to shape their growing prejudicial perspectives.

Only hours after the attacks, many of us watched the emotional rants of US citizens across the country, spewing racial and faith-based hatred indiscriminately on the entire Muslim religion, making genocidal declarations like, "They should all be killed," or "We need to go over there and wipe them off the face of the planet." Of course, people were angry and allowing their emotions to get the better of them, with many making shocking statements and taking drastic action. Some Americans even left great jobs to join the military to fight. I can't help but think many of them were seeking revenge, and jumped at the chance to deliver a little payback, rather than the larger purpose of defending our freedom. Others felt the need to do something meaningful and tangible. The normal online donation while watching *Oprah* just didn't seem like enough.

Sam Harris, author of the *End of Faith* and *Letter to a Christian Nation*, commented on how the events of 9/11 prompted him to write. He has often warned that neutrality could lead to annihilation. By not taking a stand for reason, we are allowing the unreasonable to thrive unabated.

In my opinion, most Christian Americans are honest, caring, decent people. They are unconcerned with the extreme fringes of their beliefs and very comfortable with breaking bread with anyone who shares their values. They don't care if someone's high moral standard comes from faith or family, as long as it's present in their actions. The problem is when one of their religious leaders, spokesmen or prominent figures makes an outrageously prejudicial or divisive claim, they often fail to take appropriate action. The religious moderate sometimes allows the religious fundamentalist the option of hiding behind their societal and political skirts, knowing you (the religious moderate) will defend the annihilable rights of faith, while ignoring the fundamentalist's abuse of that right, never ousting anyone who makes these unsubstantiated claims, allowing them to propagate hatred.

"But I don't agree with their crazy claims," says some of the religiously neutral. Unfortunately I sometimes think your quiet endorsement is offered by your sheer involvement. By not finding a new church home, denouncing their ridiculous claims, or voting for another candidate, you may be saying, "I support you". That tacit support gives them a perceived credibility, coercing others without your clarity of thought into adopting their religious bias.

Words have power, and because they can affect belief, and belief can assuredly affect actions, you have to watch what you say or convey. There is a reason you can't yell "Bomb" on an airplane, and it's very simple: it has the strong potential to incite people to behave in a way that might harm themselves or others. How many doctors performing legal abortion in this country have been murdered because of belief? Thanks in part to fundamentalist websites that post their personal information online? If a public figure believes God is telling him an entire race of people are evil, in league with Satan, or are following a false God, they need to keep those sentiments to themselves unless it can be backed by evidence. Your unwillingness to police these less reserved individuals within your own camp will certainly provoke others to act. Unfortunately, this might force your opposition to make broad sword strokes against your faith, instead of precision strikes. I will say it again: If religion were a simple personal pursuit, where it was not forcibly pushed on anyone else, I think it would be largely left alone. But as it stands now, the baby may have to go with the bath water, unless each belief system can maintain neutrality.

I recently visited a local museum that was showcasing relics, photos, and speakers from the Jewish holocaust that took place during World War II. I remember watching a video clip that I believe was recorded in the 1970s, in which a woman spoke about the attitudes she believed fostered the hatred that led to the holocaust. I'm taking this from memory, but I think she said, "When you demonize a people, and claim they are of a lesser God, this breeds hatred." While walking through the exhibit, I was contemplatively appalled. I was astonished at how cavalier the Nazis were towards the lives of their Jewish prisoners. Here again you have a people of a rich heritage facing amazing hardships, with Adolph Hitler attempting nothing less then genocide. Yet, the Jewish people still had faith!

This is another aspect of faith that confuses me, unwavering faith in the face of unimaginable hardships. The believer's ability to filter the most horrific experiences so only the positives are acknowledged and credited to God. We never require an explanation for why God appeared to abandon his "chosen" people during their most difficult times. Many will claim that God was always in the wings working on the behalf of the true disciples, and had not turned his back on them, but was supporting his believers and their mission. My question is which believers or mission would you be referencing?

Regardless of whether we are talking about the Crusades, Inquisitions, the continued fighting in the Middle East, or the Jewish holocaust, both sides of these conflicts had one thing in common: belief in the same God! In most cases, alleged holy men committed these acts while claiming to follow the will of the God of Abraham. While the origin stories of the three major religions and their saviors are certainly different, at the heart of the faith lies the same deity. The Nazis believed, like everyone, that they were following the one true God, and that he was asking them to stomp out the people of a false deity. This was Hitler's claim: that God placed a great responsibility on his shoulders to purge the planet of inferior races and religions. The persecutors seem to always believe they are exterminating a lesser people following a lesser God. Conversely, the persecuted always believe it to be the will of their God, that at least for a time being, their hardships are deserved and a required part of his great plan. This is always followed by the sentiment that God is omnibenevolent. "Men never do evil so completely and cheerfully as when they do it from religious conviction," philosopher Blaise Pascal once wrote.

With 9/11, we have the same circumstances. Most of the Christian world denounced the attack as a deplorable act from not only an extremist group of radical Muslims, but from a false and militant religion, going on to state that God would pull them through this tragedy, and exact revenge on Al-Qaida and Islam. However, some in the Islamic world saw the attack as a message from their God (the Same God), exacting revenge on the infidels who defiled the Muslim people and their land. Which is it? How would this have played out differently if God were not believed to be real? Unless God is an evil arms dealer providing spiritual support for both sides of the conflict, he doesn't care about either side of these issues, because he doesn't exist.

It's very difficult to talk about the change in attitude towards faith in this country without making some reference to 9/11. But the real power of this and any tragedy is the overwhelming feeling of helplessness. People flock to the church because something beyond their control has happened, and they don't know what to do. They don't know how to rationalize the senseless acts of suffering or violence. So they accept the answers given to them by their pastor and preachers, whether or not any qualifiers or evidence are

attached. For many, there is an unwavering need to make sense out
of a tragedy. They need to be able to wrap their minds around it
so they can begin to put it past them. They want to be comforted,
and are simply not willing to accept the notion that some things
happen at random or with mindless malicious intent, because that
just wouldn't be fair.

This mindset really confuses me, this idea that there must be
a strange force controlling everything; that someone or something
must be looking out for us. When I speak with my friends, there
is an unspoken sense of entitlement in being human. If something
happens to animals, they go extinct, starve to death, or get caught
in a flood, it's seen as a random event that only impacts lower life
forms. But if something happens to mankind, it can't be random.
It must be a part of some great pre-designed plan. I have even
known other Atheists who carry this same unfounded sentiment.
But I can't figure out why everyone believes there are a plethora of
unforeseen or undiscovered forces (other than powerful or greedy
humans) that govern our world, completely influenced by our
wants, needs, emotions and behaviors.

I have been continually told that life is not fair. But I don't
think everyone really grasps this concept. Because it basically
means that bad things can happen to you for no apparent reason.
You could die tomorrow and it would just be a freak accident,
and not posses any underlining meaning. We invented the concepts or labels of right and wrong, good and evil, and they did not
come with a watchdog, or omnipotent guardian to ensure their fair
dispersal! That's why life is not fair? I just don't get it. Why do
we think we must have been given a purpose that was conceived
before our birth? Or that circumstances will just work themselves
out for the better, because we want them too? Or the idea that if
you're a good person, a just reward awaits you in your future?
Or that a true love has been created specifically for you and just

awaits the perfect meeting? We believe this, even when the realities of life continually show us the contrary. So just because we want something ... Life might be easier to understand if ... You would feel better when ... It doesn't mean that it will happen, nor are you entitled to it.

Nevertheless, as soon as the next major disaster happens, I'm sure the pews will fill again, simply because we are not capable of processing a world that we cannot control. This is the real power of religion. The church seems to be a relationship of convenience for many. When the community experiences an extreme emotional low, they run into the arms of the church to be comforted and told everything will work out in God's great plan. Unfortunately, it's a false sense of security. This is so ironic, since the whole concept of faith calls for simple trust in him. I would think that the truly faithful would rejoice and take comfort in knowing that God's will has been done, and would not seek vengeance on the instruments of his will. If what you tell me is true and nothing happens that is not directed by the Almighty, then he's the one you should be angry with, show prejudice toward, or look for answers from. There would be no need to retaliate against the instruments used in his divine plan.

However, our healing process seems to consist of doing something that allows us to regain that feeling of control over our lives. So instead of working on creating peace to minimize conflicts, or inventing technology to accurately predict, counteract, or save lives during natural disasters, we just hope for change. If we were as determined to truly understand the world around us as much as we prayed to understand it, we could probably design the control that we all so desperately seem to desire, and not have to appeal to a divine authority for it.

ARE WE ALONE?

OK.. So here we go again! Hundreds of years ago, we thought the earth was flat. We were wrong. Then we thought the earth was the center of the Universe and all the planets revolved around us. Wrong again! Then we thought we must be the only earth-like planet in the habitable zone orbiting a host star. Big surprise: we are being proven wrong again. But now, we think that we must be the only intelligent life in the Universe.

Stop listening to the mouthpieces of the mass media, and start listening to the astrobiologists and physicists that study the ET potential, because they have a very different take on things. What's that you say? Life can't survive in those conditions? But haven't we found life in the deepest oceans, coldest places, hottest deserts and most acidic environments on earth? Don't extremophiles and other microscopic organisms continue to impress us with the conditions in which they can survive and thrive? Isn't that the whole point of natural selection, to favor traits that allow life to exist in their environments, no matter how hostile or extreme? Haven't we adapted to the conditions on earth and in space, and not the other way around? Don't we still suspect life might have, or still does exist in our own solar system? Doesn't science believe fossilized life on Mars, and possible aquatic life in the speculated liquid interior of Europa, might be possible? To take a quote from Jurassic Park, "Life will find a way!"

The claim that life is meaningless without GOD has always baffled me. If there were a guaranteed life after death for the faithful in God's perfect kingdom, then outside of behaving yourself for admittance into this realm, what would be the point of this earthly existence? But if the afterlife is unknown and not assured, it would instantly swell the importance of this existence. If you're right, and there is a benevolent God who loves us, would he want his greatest achievement—humanity—to render itself extinct over a disagreement regarding which ancient text is correct? But if I'm right, and there is no God or guaranteed afterlife, doesn't that make this life and us extremely unique, especially since we haven't found any other intelligent life in the Universe?

If you can't tell, I've been a science fiction fan for quite some time. This has made me dwell on the prospect of where our society is heading. As far as we know, we are completely unique to our Universe. We are the only sentient life form of which we are aware, and we continually search the stars for any other signs of life. In fact, this is one of the greatest questions ever posed by the human race… "Are we alone?"

I agree with most of the scientists and tend to think this is highly unlikely. Why? Because of the sheer vastness of space! It's so large that it's almost impossible to comprehend. Our fastest spacecraft would take centuries to reach the other side of our own Milky Way galaxy, and ours is just one galaxy amongst billions. Our moderate-sized galaxy alone contains billions upon billions of stars. This translates into trillions of planets, and the whole thing has been running for nearly 14 billion years. I know these are some very large numbers, but I'm simply trying to illustrate just how immense the Universe is, and why it would be almost a mathematical impossibility for us to be the only life in the cosmos.

Since liquid water is a key component for life on earth, that's what we look for when trying to locate ET. Which is a great idea and the logical place to start, but that doesn't necessarily mean all life followed our model. By the most conservative estimates, there should be millions of planets in what's called the "Goldilocks Zone"—not too hot, and not too cold, but just right for water to remain in its liquid form on a planet's surface. If the planet is too close to its Sun or host star, the water boils off and evaporates. Too far away, and it freezes solid. Using the now famous Drake equation, which attempts to estimate the number of sentient or intelligent civilizations in our Universe, there should be thousands in our galaxy alone. Many people think since we have been looking for ET for decades, and haven't found a thing, we must be the only life in the Cosmos. Unfortunately, with our limited technology, we haven't even begun to effectively search the Universe for life. A physicist on the Science Channel offered a very perceptive analogy for this concept. If you dip a drinking glass into the ocean and hold its lifeless contents up to the sunlight, would you say there is no life in the ocean? Or would you speculate that you haven't sampled enough of the total area to draw such a conclusion? However, if you put a drop of that ocean beneath a microscope, you would see a microscopic world teeming with life! So maybe life exists right in front of us, but we just haven't developed the tools with which to see it.

Michio Kaku, a theoretical physicist and futurist at CUNY, has frequently commented on our pivotal place in history. He wonders if humanity will make it to what he calls a Type One Civilization. Without getting to in depth, this is a global society that had reached a certain level of cultural unity and technological advancement with the ability to control their environment. It also has successfully overcome certain self-destructive societal issues that have threatened their civilization.

Which brings us to the primary reason I believe Mr. Kaku doubts our ability to reach this first threshold: the very real fear we will destroy ourselves before we solve our problems. I think this fear might be shared by a vast number of us. A few scientists have also speculated that some of the absences of intelligent life throughout the Universe might be a result of self-annihilation. Assuredly, every advanced civilization has come to the same place in their history, and in some cases made the wrong choice. Their societal maturity never kept pace with their ability to wage war on a planetary scale!

One of our greatest disadvantages as a species is the fact that the entire human race lives in this one planetary basket. If anything happens to the earth, goodbye humanity. I desperately want scientist to find some form of alien life. Anything on the smallest scale would force mankind from their self-proclaimed celestial high horse, and require us to reevaluate our whole notion regarding religion and our cosmological importance. Instantly, a million hard questions would present themselves about the uniqueness of our human condition. Discovering microbial or bacterial life would be great, but finding the equivalent of an otherworldly insect would exponentially increase the likelihood of finding intelligent civilizations to almost guaranteed certainty.

But would we be ready to meet ET? I sometimes wonder what would happen if a malevolent, opportunistic or even benevolent species found it's way to earth. Our dependency on an unseen agency, instead of our own ingenuity and resourcefulness, might leave us vulnerable or gullible. Any life form that could make it to our blue marble would be many times more advanced than us, primarily because we haven't even attained a level of technology that would allow a manned vessel to successfully leave our own solar system. If another civilization had stumbled upon mankind thousands of years ago, and needed our natural resources or minerals, they wouldn't have to enter our atmosphere with particle weapons blazing. They could simply employ technology common to their society, but eons beyond anything we have devised, and it would influence most of the population to fall to their knees.

Picture a civilization that is completely space faring, wondering through the cosmos looking for resources to maintain their ever-growing population. Once they found a planet rich in their much-needed elements, they could convince the locals to mine it for them as a simple offering to their divinity. By merely landing their crafts in plain sight, they could approach the locals and ask for anything they wanted. The sight of technologically advanced flying machines landing in the centers of communities, employing devices completely foreign to mankind, would instantly be equated to Godlike powers. Arthur C. Clarke once said, "Any significantly advanced technology is indistinguishable from magic." If they were to show up during the 21st century, they would have to do a little more work, but nothing beyond their ability. Simply by investigating our mythology, extraterrestrial visitors could convince the vast majority of us that every messiah in every civilization had returned. Or they could raise an ominous voice from the clouds, sending us scrambling for cover, fearing our all-powerful and supposedly benevolent deity had come to dispense judgment on mankind. Oddly enough, the few skeptical individuals, who would not be so easily deceived, would be labeled as blasphemers and punished severely.

Many of the arguments I've heard for all kinds of phenomena involve comparing our current level of technology or scientific understanding to a question that is beyond its ability to answer. Then we place an unfounded, speculative placeholder in the answer slot until we can find something better. Many will say, "That's the same thing we do with scientific theories." I disagree. Those theories offer one answer that is meticulously tested. That's why science or a particular theory isn't completely turned on its ear every few years. Science has devised a methodology to determine which theories will be accepted or rejected. Religion simply allows all untested claims to have equal merit based on personal opinion.

The real point, which I don't think I will ever understand about our species, is the concept that it's perfectly acceptable and widely practiced to make up a place holding, unsupported answer until we can find a better explanation. Until science has provided an unequaled or more definitive claim based on hard data, why do we get to play God? I will be the first to admit that compelling or interesting evidence exists for or against several types of phenomena, but I only see it as a mystery that needs solving. I try to never draw a conclusion until most of the pieces are in play. It's like *Wheel of Fortune*, with only one or two letters visible. The long phrase could be almost anything. However, as more information is revealed, the number of possible answers greatly decreases, until it becomes obvious to everyone what the correct answer is.

While there is nothing wrong with speculation, I sometimes think we forget that it's just the beginning of the discovery process. I just can't understand why a speculation, guess, or hunch is presented as a fact, conclusion or law. If your evidence points to multiple explanations, I don't understand why you wouldn't be required to provide reasons for choosing one answer over another, before passing it along as a certainty. This is the only point I'm trying to make. Reserve judgment until all the facts are in, be humbled by our inability to answer the big questions, and not intimidated by its complexity to jump to hasty unsupported conclusions.

So why is this a big deal, why cant we just go on believing and spreading anything that is comfortable? Because the average person seems to be so impressionable, rarely investigating information for themselves. This is the power of the scam, misinformation campaigns, and the birth of the conspiracy theory. If someone watches a Youtube video on a scintillating piece of information that a company, government, or secret society is assumed to be hiding, another conspiracy theorist is born, often jumping to conclusions without any collaborating evidence. When you ask, "Why do they believe this claim over any other, when the information was presented in identical formats?" they don't have an answer. We believe the eyewitness accounts of Bigfoot, but not of the Loch Ness Monster. We believe Aliens are going to show themselves on a particular date. When nothing happens, it's just reasoned away, or the subsequent date is pushed back.

After watching one side of an argument, many seem to go out and perpetuate unconfirmed information as the truth. Does it mean they are wrong? Of course not! I strongly believe that in some circumstances, the people controlling the spread of information are purposely hiding or withholding the very evidence that could validate a particular claim. I just think we need to be very careful about spreading potentially dangerous hearsay. Does that mean I personally research everything in my life from who made the T-shirt I'm wearing to the alleged structures on Mars? Of course not. But I'm also not pushing a message or agenda about these topics, either.

For example, many believe we have already been visited by alien life, and that the government is hiding the evidence of extra terrestrial visitation from the general public. In all honesty, I understand why this idea prevails, mainly due to the government's weak official position on particular UFO claims. If they would simply give a more plausible explanation for strange events, and not maintain that dozens of people that witnessed an unidentified cigar or triangular shaped craft, of enormous size, adorned with strange lights, performing maneuvers beyond the scope of any known craft, was not just a weather balloon, meteor, or strange cloud formation, I think more people would believe them.

Now I'm certainly not saying ET is here and visiting us. I just think some of the explanations provided by the media can be ridiculous. Is our government hiding information regarding UFOs? Of course they are, if only to hide the existence of super-secret experimental aircraft. But even if they were hiding proof of Alien's visitations, why shouldn't they?

I've heard conspiracy theorists asking for full disclosure about the perceived Extra Terrestrials cover-up. But I can't help but wonder, what's in it for the governments of the world? What purpose would it serve? Think about it. What would happen if our President said we had been in contact with an alien race, or found evidence of complex life on another planet? Couldn't this information potentially throw our civilization out of whack? More than two-thirds of the people in this country believe there is a God, who created the Universe completely for us, and everyone must go through Jesus to get into heaven. Could we continue to maintain this arrogant assertion that the Universe was designed for our species alone? Suddenly belief systems around the world would have millions of hard questions to answer. Furthermore, since many Christians vehemently maintain that their beliefs strengthen them, and provide them purpose, hope and guidance through life, wouldn't proof of ET represent a challenge to those longstanding beliefs? Without working answers to these newly posed questions, how would they reconcile this new information? How would that affect our way of life? How many science fiction programs have we watched in which the leader of a society hides the evidence of interplanetary visitation, solely because the general public was unready to emotionally handle the realization that they were not the only intelligence in the Universe?

But let's forget the religious implications for a moment. There would be far more pressing questions that would need immediate answers if ET decided to pay us a visit. Are they friendly? Why are they here? What information are they willing to share? Who gets to interact with them? If a spacecraft lands on the White House lawn, would our country represent all mankind to the ET's? What about the possible acquisition of advanced medicines or technology? Would they be shared equally?

Given the ambitious, power hungry nature of some world leaders, I wouldn't be surprised if they hoarded any technology or miracle medicines for themselves! At the risk of sounding like a conspiracy theorist myself, or a science fiction author, why wouldn't the people in the "know" simply reverse engineer a few advance components every few decades? Slowly introducing them to the population, being careful not to saturate the market too quickly and draw suspicion. Maybe they would simply take alien cures to longstanding earthly diseases and dilute them into expensive treatments that would generate billions. What was the last major illness our civilization eradicated from our planet? However, we have certainly been able to discover many interesting ailments that require new drugs whose side effects appear worse than the illness it was meant to treat.

Ultimately, if I were a leader, I would most likely never disclose the presence of extraterrestrial life until I felt my religious or superstitious citizens could emotionally and physiologically handle the truth. Since I would have been elected to preserve their way of life, why would I make an announcement that carries the potential to destroy it? Because many allow their emotions to dictate their actions, even in the absence of evidence, and since common sense appears not to be all that common, I think I would keep quite a bit from the masses.

In the original *Men in Black*, "J" (Will Smith) asked "K" (Tommy Lee Jones), "Why don't you just tell people (the truth about aliens), they are smart, they can handle it!"

"K" responded, "A person is smart. People are dumb, panicky, dangerous animals, and you know it!"

So how could we protect citizens from themselves? How could we keep the truth from the immature masses, and the inquisitive ones that are actually awake! Easy: by creating the perception that ET is a myth, legend, is only for the weak-minded. The news organizations and media would trivialize and joke about UFO claims, making it appear that only fanatics and unstable personalities believed in that kind of phenomena. I would have secret bases, like the infamous "Area 51" in Nevada, in which I could conduct experiments that were off limits to the public, where deadly force would be authorized against any trespassers. Because these reverse-engineered prototype aircraft would need to be tested, I would ensure that any pilots that spoke about seeing an unidentified flying object would be ridiculed and lose their licenses, forcing them to keep their sightings to themselves. On the rare occasions when I was compelled or felt the need share declassified documents to the masses, I would black out the portions I didn't want anyone to read.

But the reality is I don't have to give an explanation for anything. I can simply claim that any location, information, documentation, footage, or paten has been seized or deemed off limits in the interest of national security. That is the government's ultimate trump card of last resort. This would also ensure that I could maintain secrecy about any alien or UFO interaction or information that would personally benefit myself, or my agendas. But again, this is a hypothetical scenario, and would be a better plot for a science fiction novel, than a headline in the local newspaper.

In the interest of being impartial, I once asked myself, "Am I being hypocritical by carrying a belief that alien life must exist, while insisting that this entity known as God does not?"

I think this answer is based on scope. That is, scope of the Alien claim pressed against the God claim.

Over 95% of all life that has ever existed on this planet is extinct, and yet billions of examples of life still exist today. This seems to suggest that while life forms, and even species can be fragile and may die off from time-to-time, the state of life itself is the most virulent thing we have ever come across. Killing a cockroach is easy, wiping out the entire species appears to be impossible! On our planet, life has spanned billions of years, existed in billions of species, surviving planet wide climate changes, asteroid impacts, and Volcanism. Every time we go deeper into the ocean, further into the desserts, or uncover another subterranean cavern, we find life. Given its apparent sentient nature to survive, what justification do we have to simply assume life couldn't have found a way somewhere else in the Universe?

At the end of the day, why am I so comfortable with the notion of alien life vs. God life? Because belief in this very scientifically grounded hypothesis only observes the facts, and makes a logical conclusion from there. It doesn't make outlandish claims without evidence. It simply sees the limitless enormity of the Cosmos, mated to the prolifically creative, omnipotent nature of life and says, yeah, mathematically that had to happen somewhere else. Not to mention this claim can also be satisfied by the simplest forms of life. This is why we quarantine Astronauts when they come back from outer space, because we want the Andromeda strain to remain a science fiction movie.

Unfortunately, the God claims are enormously outrages, requiring an insurmountable amount of evidence to support its unsubstantiated claims. Postulating that something might be crawling across a planet's surface light years away from earth, is not crazy when we have seen a plethora of examples right here on earth. But the idea that there is a being that can do, see, or is involved in everything, everywhere, would require a colossal amount of remarkable evidence, especially when not a single attribute has ever been proven.

I also like the fact that finding life, out there, doesn't have to affect my daily life, down here. If the Mars rover curiosity came face to face with a strange, short gray alien, with spindly limbs and an unusually large head with big black eyes, it doesn't have to change how I treat my neighbor. There won't be any claims that this alien wrote a binding doctrine, has a particular perspective of earthly tragedies, or believes one ancient group of people were inherently better than another. It will simply be a discovery that needs investigation. Sure it will profoundly affect mankind's self-proclaimed cosmological importance, but hopefully just the knowledge wouldn't divide us into factions. On further thought, maybe I'm giving humanity too much credit, because we have an amazing capacity to diligently search for, and expertly find the differences in us, while purposely ignoring the easily observed commonalities.

On the other side of the coin, president Ronald Reagan once said, "In our obsession with antagonism of the moment, we often forget how much unites the members of humanity. Perhaps we need some outside, universal threat to make us recognize this common bond. I occasionally think how quickly our differences worldwide would vanish if we were facing an alien threat from outside this world."

At our present level of societal maturity, I sometimes wonder if the instantaneous knowledge of intelligent life in the Universe might become a double-edged sword. Would it drive us forward? Or crazy? Would it bind our civilization against a common outsider, unite us in celebration, or further divide us over the potential spoils?

Christian Nation

I hear it in the media, from people on the streets and from politicians all the time, but I have yet to understand the phrase: "We are a Christian Nation and we should return to the good Christian values this country was founded on." Since the Constitution is considered the law-establishing blueprint for our nation, I figured it would be the only logical place to alleviate my confusion. Unfortunately, when I researched this all-inclusive document and the people responsible for its inception, I was unsure about how it supported the notion that we are a Christian nation.

I first assumed the idea of a National Christian heritage came from the religious example given by our forefathers. I assumed their faith-based morality was a clear continual presence in the Constitution, and their religious philosophies were principles we needed to return to. However, when I researched the beliefs of the influential founding fathers, many could have been considered agnostics or deists, not theists! This was very evident in their treatment and wording of the document they came together to create. First and foremost, the word "God" or phrase "Christian Nation" does not appear anywhere in this all-important text.

In fact, the very first amendment states, *"Congress shall make no law respecting an establishment of religion, or prohibiting the free exercise thereof."* The establishment clause also prohibits Congress from showing preference to one religion over another, or over non-belief. Another rare reference to religion in the Constitution refers to an idea introduced by Charles Pinckney: "No religious test shall ever be required as a qualification to any office or public trust under the United States."

So basically, the government cannot prohibit someone of a particular religion, or non-religion, from holding any publicly elected seat. You would think a devoutly Christian group, as many modern-day Christians regard the Founding Fathers, would have taken this opportunity to shape the philosophical, ethical and religious foundation of our country any way they saw fit. Why wouldn't they have declared us a Christian nation? Why didn't they require belief in the Christian God as a requirement for eligibility to run for public office? Why didn't they season the Constitution with scriptures to send a very clear message about which faith represents our nation?

The simple answer is they didn't want to, because they were not all Christians, and recognized the divisive nature of religion, as well as the variety and personal nature of spiritual beliefs. But don't take my word for it. The following quotes are from our founding fathers regarding their religious convictions, or lack there of:

Thomas Paine

"I do not believe in the creed professed by the Jewish Church, by the Roman Church, by the Greek Church, by the Turkish Church, by the Protestant Church, nor by any Church that I know of. My own mind is my own Church." (From *The Age of Reason*)

"Take away from Genesis the belief that Moses was the author, on which only the strange belief that it is the word of

God has stood, and there remains nothing of Genesis but an anonymous book of stories, fables, and traditional or invented absurdities, or of downright lies." (From *The Age of Reason*)

"The Bible is a book that has been read more and examined less than any book that ever existed." (From *The Theological Works of Thomas Paine*)

"Priests and conjurors are of the same trade." (From *The Age of Reason*)

Benjamin Franklin

"Some books against Deism fell into my hands; they were said to be the substance of sermons preached at Boyle's Lectures. It happened that they wrought an effect on me quite contrary to what was intended by them; for the arguments of the Deists, which were quoted to be refuted, appeared to me much stronger than the refutations; in short, I soon became a thorough Deist." (From *Benjamin Franklin Biography*)

"I have found Christian dogma unintelligible. Early in life I absented myself from Christian assemblies. (From *Ben Franklin*, Poor Richard's Almanack, *1758*)

"The way to see by faith is to shut the eye of reason: The Morning Daylight appears plainer when you put out your Candle." (From *Ben Franklin*, Poor Richard's Almanack, *1758*)

"Lighthouses are more helpful than churches." (From *Ben Franklin*, Poor Richard's Almanack, *1758*)

John Adams

"As I understand the Christian religion, it was, and is, a revelation. But how has it happened that millions of fables, tales, legends, have been blended with both Jewish and Christian revelation that have made them the most bloody religion that ever existed?" (From *a letter to F.A. Van der Kamp, Dec. 27, 1816*)

Thomas Jefferson

"Christianity neither is, nor ever was, a part of the common law. " (*Thomas Jefferson letter to Dr. Thomas Cooper, 1814*)

"The day will come when the mystical generation of Jesus, by the Supreme Being as his father, in the womb of a virgin, will be classed with the fable of the generation of Minerva in the brain of Jupiter." (From *a letter to John Adams, April 11, 1823*)

James Madison

"The Civil Government, though bereft of everything like an associated hierarchy, possesses the requisite stability, and performs its functions with complete success, whilst the number, the industry, and the morality of the priesthood, and devotion of the people, have been manifestly increased by the total separation of the church from the state." (*James Madison in a letter to Robert Walsh, March 2, 1819*)

"Religious bondage shackles and debilitates the mind and unfits it for every noble enterprise, every expanded prospect." (*James Madison in a letter to William Bradford, April 1, 1774*)

Strangely enough, these don't sound like the words of a devoutly religious group that viewed Christianity as the guiding faith of their fledgling nation. Consider the fact that they could not resolve the issue of slavery, but were perfectly fine reaching a consensus to exclude religious belief from the Constitution, which leads me to believe it was not omitted by accident.

Thomas Jefferson was one of the first to introduce the idea that the Church body and the governing bodies of government should remain divided. In a letter he wrote to the Danberry Baptist Association, he highlighted this importance with the phrase "Wall of separation between the church and state," which was later shortened to "separation of church and state." He firmly held the notion that religious belief was a very personal matter between the individual and whatever God they professed to believe in, and in no way should a government meant to represent all the people take sides in a personal matter that would surely divide the people. Even in our dealings with other countries, we were quick to distance ourselves from the "Christian Nation" perception. The Treaty of Tripoli that president John Adams submitted to the Senate in early 1797, and was unanimously ratified later that year, clearly stated,

"As the Government of the United States of America is not, in any sense, founded on the Christian religion; as it has in itself no character of enmity against the laws, religion, or tranquility, of Mussulmen; and, as the said States never entered into any war or act of hostility against any Mahometan nation, it is declared by the parties that no pretext arising from religious opinions shall ever produce an interruption of the harmony existing between the two countries."

What about the "In God We Trust" motto emblazoned on every dollar bill, or the "One Nation under God" statement within the Pledge of Allegiance? Interestingly enough, the motto "In God We Trust" was challenged in court, in Aronow vs. United States in 1970. It was argued as a clear violation of the constitutional clause I quoted earlier, which prohibits the government from establishing a national religion or endorsing one religion over another. The United States Court of Appeals for the Ninth Circuit ruled:

"It is quite obvious that the national motto and the slogan on coinage and currency 'In God We Trust' has nothing whatso-

ever to do with the establishment of religion. Its use is of patri-otic or ceremonial character and bears no true resemblance to a governmental sponsorship of a religious exercise."

Yet, this motto is often offered as first evidence that we are a Christian nation, even when the court has clearly stated it to be nothing more than a patriotic or ceremonial character. So which is it? Is it a clear endorsement of Christianity as the national religion, thus violating constitutional law and should be subject to removal from all US currency? Or is it just a colorful use of language pro-moting national pride and in no way establishes the United States as a Christian Nation?

"One Nation Under God" was added to the Pledge of Alle-giance in 1954, to make a distinction between Americans and the Godless Communist, members of Congress said at the time. In 2000, Atheist Michael Newdow challenged the phrase, claiming it was a violation of the separation of church and state. When it was first brought to the San Francisco-based 9th U.S. Circuit Court of Appeals in 2002, they ruled in favor of Mr. Newdow, stating the phrase violated the constitutional expectation that prohibits the government sanctioning of a particular religion.

This decision caused an unprecedented amount of backlash from the Christian community, and a political shockwave that led President George W. Bush to call the ruling ridiculous. After several years and appeals, the case was later rejected in a 2-1 vote. Proceeding over that case was Judge Carlos Bea, who was quoted as saying, "The Pledge of Allegiance serves to unite our vast nation through the proud recitation of some of the ideals upon which our Republic was founded." But I don't understand why it's okay to cherry pick and recite the ideals we personally like from that time period. Why don't we recite the ideals to slavery, or misogyny, since the republic was also founded under such principles?

Incidentally, Mr. Bea was appointed by President Bush. Why is this significant? Because our former president once said God told him to invade Iraq. His father, George H. W. Bush, said, "Atheists are neither citizens nor patriots."

While I personally believe these kinds of remarks have no place in the language of someone who has been elected to uphold the rights and privileges of all Americans, not just the Christian ones, I do admire their strong convictions and desire to stand behind them. I just would think becoming a church pastor might have been a better outlet for those sentiments.

The real issue with the "Christian Nation" claim lies with the people in the Christian majority that don't care if it's right or wrong, if its backed by legal documents, or if it violates someone else's rights. It's simply what they prefer, even when they would never accept anyone asking their children to recite the name of another God. Furthermore, any elected official that does not abide by their expectations are subject to being voted out of office and their political career at a minimum, and in worse case scenarios, they can receive death threats from the most extreme in the ideology.

"But Ron, again I say we are a Christian nation," still says many. Fine, but you haven't proven that outside of simply asserting that the preponderance of Americans identify themselves as Christians. This is simply a plea from majority. How do we ignore the fact that no one in any official position uses this claim as a valid argument?

Why didn't the judges presiding over those controversial cases simply say, "We are a Christian nation, and that's why it's okay for the motto to be on the coins, or for 'Under God' to be in the Pledge of Allegiance," and leave it at that? Because they knew it would be an outright violation of what the Founding Fathers stated in the Constitution. So they merely underplayed the importance and impact of the words as lively idioms paying homage to an earlier time, knowing that the everyday Christian not bound by these constitutional restraints would espouse the real message they privately endorse. Fortunately, or unfortunately (depending on your beliefs), I can't find a single document or binding legislation signed by any president or branch of government that officially affiliates our country with any particular system of faith. Until you can find such a legal precedent to support the claim that we are a "Christian Nation," there will be opposition from a growing population with differing religious beliefs.

With that said, I freely admit that the majority of our citizens consider themselves Christians; maybe that's the point: Government by the people for the people. With that in mind, I guess we have a choice to make. Either our elected officials will amend the Constitution so we are legally considered a Christian nation, and favoring that particular religion would not be an area of disagreement. Or, we dismiss every claim of faith-based discrimination, and work diligently to achieve religious neutrality throughout the country, removing any governmental or public school affiliation with a specific system of belief. While the first option might seem appealing to most, I urge you to consider the floodgate of repressive legislation that could follow. Less than a century ago, women couldn't vote. Until the first Gulf War, they couldn't fight in the military, and they still aren't paid the same as men, in many professions. Would a nationwide religious declaration, aligning us to Christianity and excluding all other faiths, stop there? Would we be forced to cater to any national trait represented by the clear majority? Would we also be considered a white or female nation as well?

What kind of message would that send to the rest of the world? Would foreign policy suddenly be dictated by someone's personal interpretation of Christian scriptures, or private communications from God? Would we treat Muslim countries more harshly or with less respect than Christian ones? Would we be painting a big red bull's-eye on our head, encouraging extremist groups to work harder than ever to overthrow a country that has publicly declared itself a Christian nation? Would elected officials create laws that would only favor their system of faith?

Our secular government protects the religious freedom of all Americans. Unfortunately, many don't care about the religious freedoms of the masses, as long as their faith isn't being oppressed. During the 2010 Christmas holiday in Iraq, an extremist group was responsible for killing Christians in a local church. But since Iraq is more than 90 percent Muslim, shouldn't it be considered an Islamic nation in the same way that the United States would be considered a Christian nation? Furthermore, the Iraqi constitution clearly declares Islam as the recognized religion and basic foundation of the country's laws. No such declaration was ever penned into our Constitution, and yet many feel perfectly fine declaring the United States a Christian nation. So should Christians who live in a clearly Muslim country, which has openly aligned itself to the specific religion of Islam, convert or leave? Or do you believe they should have the religious freedom to practice as they see fit?

We call ourselves the great melting pot as a testament to our diversity, and yet we are not willing to equally honor the richness of our cultural mix. Why should people of differing beliefs share your sense of national pride if their faith is considered the underclass of belief, not worth mentioning, and restricted to the specific halls where they are practiced? While Christianity is considered the religious royalty of our society, enjoying freedoms the other faiths could only hope for? Where Christian prayers are commonplace in most public areas, where every school or judicial building is adorned with only Christian scriptures and paraphernalia?

So much for the separation of church and state.

When I speak to Christians about how they would feel about Islamic symbolism, ideology, or signage adorning public facilities, they grow outraged. Yet, they are shocked when they realize others feel the same way about the Christian faith. Shouldn't a government that requires taxes and provides for all its citizens remain neutral in its treatment of religious faith? Doesn't it make sense that everyone should be allowed to enjoy religious freedom without public facilities and governing bodies taking sides? Shouldn't Christian prayers, plaques and religious material be limited to the churches and private schools that acknowledge those affiliations?

The reality is this prevailing bias is to be expected when elected officials show partiality to their own beliefs. While reading the news online, I noticed the newly appointed governor of Alabama came under fire when in his inaugural address he said, "Anybody here today who has not accepted Jesus Christ as their savior, I'm telling you, You're not my brother and you're not my sister, and I want to be your brother." While he has since apologized, and I believe it was sincerely accepted by all, hasn't the damage already been done? Hasn't he made his religious prejudice so clear, can it be assumed, his official decisions as governor will be filtered through a very specific lens? Will he realistically fight as hard to uphold religious freedoms for all Alabamians, or just the Christians ones?

There has always been one thing that has really confused me about the concern regarding what our Founding Fathers would have wanted for our blossoming society. Why are we obligated to follow their moral model more than two centuries after they signed the Constitution? I'm not sure why we often act as though our Founding Fathers were godlike, wielding omniscience through their signatures, as if cut from a divine cloth. They were just people, like you and me, with the same faults and personal frailties present in all of us. The idea that they should continue to guide a social and political landscape that they could have never envisioned is odd to me.

My mother was 40 years my senior. She grew up in a very different time. This shaped her perception of our society. If she were alive today, she would be in here 80's, and would not be standing in line at the Apple Store, to grab the latest iPhone, so she could sync it to her Mac to tweet about her day and how eagerly she's waiting the release of the next *Avengers* movie. I don't think my mother had sent many text massages, knew what a Tweet was, or had ever heard of "Thor!" Virtually every social, political, technical, environmental, and spiritual issue has changed since my mother was my age, some drastically, some barley. So her perceptions of our changing society can often be old-fashioned and sometimes obsolete. So I don't understand why the beliefs of a group of men almost 250 years out of touch, should be dictating 21st century world view? Let's also not forget that many of the Founding Fathers owned slaves and endorsed its institution, openly opposing its abolishment while collaborating on the Constitution. Many did not believe in women's equality nor their right to vote. Would you trust the opinion of someone who believed owning another human being as property was perfectly acceptable? If you want to claim the forefathers were Christians, why didn't their superior morality and divine discernment tell them that slavery, segregation, and misogyny were wrong?

I'm just not inclined or feel obligated to cater to the sometimes skewed morality of a collection of men who are so out of touch. My only motivation would be to introduce and uphold legislation that would be fair and consistent to all of the people in today's society. To me, this is akin to the Civil Rights Movement.

After a change in beliefs and attitudes, we removed the signs that prohibited blacks from eating at the same diners, using the same restrooms, or drinking from the same water fountains as their white counterparts.

The social climate is changing again. Agnosticism and Atheism are growing, as well as the belief in Gods other than the Christian one. So yes, it's time to observe that we are a great nation with varying religious beliefs, and either pay tribute to them all equally and fairly—or none at all!

REVELATION

The Book of Revelation is debatably the most controversial book of the Bible, graphically outlining end-time events and ways to recognize their appearance. Unfortunately, many people believe these signs are present in today's civilization. I say unfortunately, because the belief that utter annihilation is inevitable and ordained by a divine force will influence many against taking the necessary steps to change this believed destiny. Blind faith guides the faithful to act blindly. Our species needs to understand that we, and not a God in the sky, hold the key to our destiny. While I agree we see famine, super storms, wars and rumors of wars across our world that seemingly match some supposed signs in the last book of the divine text. I certainly don't believe it's prophetic, or magical. People have been foretelling and predicting the end of days for hundreds of years, each prophetic, self-proclaimed man of God pointed to the calamities affecting their society during their own time period as definitive proof of an impending apocalypse. For example, the Crusades served as another time period supposedly meeting all the criteria of the end time prophecy.

While writing my first draft of this chapter, May 21, 2011 came and went. On that day, it was speculated the Christian

messiah would return. Bulletin boards even sprang up on inter-
states from North Carolina to California, all proclaiming that the
end time was near, or that the messiah was about to return. Of
course, nothing happened, but I was surprised that there weren't
more churches standing in opposition of this prediction. Some
even held special services on Saturday, I assume as a precaution
against the imminent doom, but never openly denounced or supported the prediction. However, if bombs had fallen, or the zombie
apocalypse began on that faithful day, I'm sure every Christian
across the globe would have jumped on the evangelical bandwagon and claimed they knew it all along!

I don't understand why people of faith are continually allowed
to guess the dates of the supposed end time, and receive a pass if
it's wrong. Why are they allowed to keep tossing out prophetic
dates, until they interpret something as fitting their guess? Even
when the Bible clearly states that no man will know the day or
the hour of the end time. When, and if a global catastrophe ever
threatens mankind, it will be documented and seen as foretold by
the religious utilizing the same foolproof method they have been
using for centuries...writing it down after it happens, or on the
day of the event, simply manipulating scripture for the less than
perfect match.

There will eventually be a worldwide incident that will greatly
affect the majority of people on our planet and potentially change
our way of life. But should this not be expected? Consider the fact
that global warming and climate change are affecting our planet
in ways unseen by any humans in thousands of years. Scientific
models suggest super storms will become super common. Our
planet has a %100 chance of being realistically threatened by a
celestial body a mile in diameter. Our dangerously addictive pursuit of power and wealth superses all morality. Religion continues
to be the most divisive construct of man's creation, mated to our

current volatile nature and growing population with apparently diminishing natural resources. Our current global climate does not seem that unexpected, and I certainly don't need a crystal ball to know things will grow progressively worse if fundamental changes aren't made. But like most religions, they wait for the definitive event, and then with Bibles thrown skyward, proclaim a loving but angry God has shown us his power. I will never understand the logic that allows people to shamelessly claim that any global catastrophe is the result of a vengeful God dispensing punishment, yet also claim he is the ultimate source of good will, especially when these indiscriminant disasters take the lives of innocent children, animals, and plant life.

By some models, the super volcano beneath Yellowstone National Park might be overdue for an eruption, if it blows its top tomorrow, and wipes out most of humanity. Christians around the world will declare it's the wrath of God. They will ignore the previous eruptions in antiquity that didn't directly involve us, or that the subsequent eruption was inevitable and/or past due. However, I hate to use the word "inevitable," because I'm still confident science will find a way of manually relieving the pressure building in that caldera, and hopefully buy us a few more centuries.

Some Christians believe the last book of the Bible is a literal warning, while others claim it's simply full of literary metaphors and must be interpreted wisely. With these two schools of thought, they have cast a wide theological net giving unwarranted credence to supposedly prophetic passages like the one claiming the world will be consumed by fire. This, of course, could point to the Yellowstone event, nuclear war, cosmic ray bombardment, Asteroid collision, the burning of fossil fuels and its affect on the environment, or something entirely more vague, like the fever associated with a pandemic. Sky, literally sky, becomes the limit as the 21st century unfolds.

From my perspective, at the risk of being overly offensive, and from a place of sheer frustration, I will close with the following rant on how I now view religious belief:

At an early age, you're indoctrinated in the Christian faith. God, Jesus, and the whole biblical ideology are presented as the only way to the truth and the light! Because it's a sin, you're taught to never question your heavenly father or the coveted belief system. At this point, the explanation of hell begins as a trite tale where parents simply explain it as a naughty place where bad little boys and girls go if they don't eat their vegetables, tell lies, or fail to clean their rooms. But as young adults these stories quickly swell to a place of eternal damnation and torture, where your soul is forever tormented for your earthly transgressions. A malevolent force bent on man's destruction, answering to many names like the Devil, Lucifer, Beelzebub, Prince of Darkness, Satan, and in his human form, the Antichrist, rules this underworld. Apparently, an omniscient and perfect God created an unsatisfied and imperfect evil Angel that he later banished to hell. But not before this most evil one waged a credible assault against a supposedly omnipotent being.

With a misshapen appearance of a genetic experiment gone wrong, the Devil employs mischievous spirits, demons, and his second-to-god omnipotence as instruments for pain and suffering. Because of his purported evil nature, to this day he is used as the supernatural scapegoat when humanity is faced with its greatest calamities and atrocities.

Despite its contradictions, plagiarized origins, period specific archaic opinions, extremely long turnaround time, and filled with the writings of reclusive or arguably power hungry men with their own agendas, the Bible is proclaimed to be the greatest literary work in history. Unfortunately, this holy book is continually flaunted as some of the only documented proof of the life of the savior and his divinity. It also regrettably serves as a much-manipulated doctrine that has meant uniquely different things to so many people, and is still used to condone prejudice, hatred, violence and death in our 21st century society! Where its constituents have made a science out of cherry-picking God's holy words, carefully ignoring the unpalatable or unexplainable portions, because that's just not how the believer wants to view God. For that matter, God is touted as an all-powerful, all-knowing, all-present deity that cannot be smelled, touched or tasted, but can only be seen through his obscure, haphazardly granted miracles or heavenly involvement, that possess no underlying pattern and aren't confined to a specific religion, group, or ideology; where he's often forced to manipulate you or others to complete the supposedly miraculous tasks. He can also be heard through the personally interpreted non-descript whispers from the dark, which of course can only be perceived by the individual.

God is also explained as perfect, and the embodiment of love, a wonderfully compassionate heavenly father whose grace knows no boundaries, who cannot stand to be in the presence of evil and does not share any of our emotional imperfections. But at the same time, through his own words, we see a self-proclaimed jealous entity, persistently unforgiving and constantly controlling of his alleged proudest creation. He has been responsible for deaths of men, women, children, as well as condoning animal sacrifice. He habitually and unjustly has held men responsible for the crimes of their bloodline, and who's vengeful nature has seen more than its fair share of collateral damage. Throughout the holy work of fiction, the continual intolerant assertion is made that homosexuality is an abomination, repeatedly typecast as one of humanity's greatest evils. But he conveniently and idly stands by while little boys are incessantly abused by supposedly the most anointed men among us, in which the guilty are continually assisted, ignored, and through contributory sin pardoned by his highest-ranking believers in our society.

Meanwhile, women are considered a subservient Garden of Eden afterthought, whose primary worth resides in their sexuality and ability to produce male offspring. From the words in his own text, God appears to be a power-abusing, powerfully abusive authority, purposely inflicting the innocent for his own unforeseen reasons, who indiscriminately uses plague, war and most importantly fear as vehicles for change, who requires continual praise and worship to feed a narcissistic personality, belief in no gods before him, no graven images, or the misuse of his name to be among the ten greatest edicts that should be passed down throughout the ages, while on occasion, seeing the need to spitefully and utterly wipe out our entire planetary ecosystem!

With the foundation of your belief system firmly intact, through example, you are given the guidelines of how to perceive your surroundings to reinforce and cement these ideas. During this entire religious maturation, your strong sense of family and community is centered on faith, where what's expected is a clear continual message. Every time the religious expectation is questioned, it's met with unusually high levels of opposition. Coincidence, luck, and random events are completely rejected and replaced with the behavior-controlling ideas like karma and the golden rule. Where phrases like "Everything happens for a reason," "Good things come to those who wait," "Patience is a virtue," and "God may not come on your time, but he is always right on time" become your constant mantras.

As you mature, so do these beliefs, and because random events don't exist and everything happens for a reason, you are left to scrutinize every key experience in your life for its underlying meaning. Unfortunately, this analysis is done with a biased psyche, filtered through the inflexible lens of faith. This, of course, is totally and absolutely unperceived. So you create artificial meanings and significance behind otherwise innocuous events. Strange feelings, soft sounds, arbitrary stimuli and random happenings become examples of God's deliberate will and intervention in your life. Any good event must have been orchestrated through God's grace, and any bad event was certainly the work of Satan. God working in mysterious ways that are simply beyond your understanding or your omniscient educator has a lesson to be learned so better decisions can be made. This is reinforced by careful fellowship with like-minded individuals who, through tradition and the same system of brainwashing, overemphasize the importance of each circumstance, all-the while ignoring obvious and pertinent questions about every situation simply because it goes against everything you've ever been taught. Not to mention the societal mandate that religious faith must be shown sensitivity regardless of how unproven, strange, or even dangerous the dogma might be. With a sense of duty to your traditions, and the fear of hell and damnation vehemently subjugating reasonable thought, you completely disregard issues of logic and reason as they pertain to your coveted belief system, systematically regurgitating the same unsubstantiated nonsense to your children and new disciples you were fed through your own religious walk.

While some of you might have doubts, which may have even grown to non-belief, the fear associated with this public life-changing announcement, coupled by the witnessed social isolation for other non-believers, has kept you silent. So you hide your skepticism and simply pretend to be a believer. This very learned trepidation has acted like a ball-and-chain, forever keeping you in the bondage of faith. Many have told you the greatest trick the Devil ever played was making people believe he never existed. But I would argue the greatest detriment to any troubled society is the unmitigated belief that an imaginary evil force is the primary reason for their very real man-made suffering. But maybe you're right. Maybe the Devil is alive and well. However, he has never existed in the form you thought he did. He's the mindset that has kept us from progressing beyond superstition. He's the tradition and ignorance that has diverted us from combating our very real man-made problems. He's the cultural unquestioned norm that has, and is, passing this curse of religious complacency, bigotry, and exclusivity from generation to generation, completely cloaked in the guise of faith, honor, and societal assumptions. While the issue of hope is a valid one, especially to a global society that appears to be continually in its care, we need to find that tangible communal strength that lives in our neighbors and loved ones to keep hope alive.

While there will always be great questions in need of answers, let's stay in the pursuit for truth, and jettison the assumptions. Let's study, theorize and intelligently categorize through facts and figures, not ostracize the masses based on supposition, superstitions and fear, because ultimately fear leads to mistrust and mistrust to hate.

Why is this such a big deal? Because we, meaning our species, are at a crossroads. No, wait! That sounds too safe. We are standing at a precipice! With one wrong move plunging us to our deaths! Am I being overly dramatic? Or eventually, will someone of a conflicting belief, inebriated by faith and obsessed with the uncompromisingly aggressive spread of their ideology, bring about a global conflict aided by 21st century weapons of mass destruction, with the simple intent of exterminating their enemies identified by doctrine?

THE END

New Falcon Publications
Publisher of Controversial Books and CDs
Invites You to Visit Our Website:
http://www.newfalcon.com

At the Falcon website you can:

- Browse the online catalog of all our great titles, including books by Robert Anton Wilson, Christopher S. Hyatt, Israel Regardie, Aleister Crowley, Timothy Leary, Osho, Lon Milo DuQuette, and many more

- Find out what's available and what's out of stock

- Get special discounts

- Order our titles through our secure online server

- Find products not available anywhere else including:
  - One of a kind and limited availability products
  - Special packages
  - Special pricing

- And much, much more